D1234080

Dedications & Other Darkhorses

Lost in the Bonewheel Factory

Copacetic

I Apologize for the Eyes in My Head

Toys in a Field

Dien Cai Dau

February in Sydney

Magic City

Neon Vernacular: New and Selected Poems

Thieves of Paradise

Blue Notes: Essays, Interviews, and Commentaries

Talking Dirty to the Gods

Pleasure Dome: New and Collected Poems

Taboo: The Wishbone Trilogy, Part One

Gilgamesh: A Verse Play

Warhorses

The Chameleon Couch

The Emperor of Water Clocks

EVERYDAY MOJO SONGS OF EARTH

NEW AND

SELECTED POEMS,

2001–2021

FARRAR STRAUS GIROUX

NEW YORK

YUSEF KOMUNYAKAA

EVERYDAY

MOJO

SONGS

OF

EARTH

Farrar, Straus and Giroux
120 Broadway, New York 10271

Copyright © 2021 by Yusef Komunyakaa
All rights reserved
Printed in the United States of America
First edition, 2021

Library of Congress Cataloging-in-Publication Data
Names: Komunyakaa, Yusef, author.
Title: Everyday mojo songs of Earth : new and selected poems, 2001–2021 /
   Yusef Komunyakaa.
Description: First edition. | New York : Farrar, Straus and Giroux, 2021. |
   Includes index.
Identifiers: LCCN 2020042798 | ISBN 9780374600136 (hardcover)
Subjects: LCGFT: Poetry.
Classification: LCC PS3561.O455 E94 2021 | DDC 811/.54—dc23
LC record available at https://lccn.loc.gov/2020042798

Designed by Crisis

Our books may be purchased in bulk for promotional, educational,
or business use. Please contact your local bookseller or the Macmillan
Corporate and Premium Sales Department at 1-800-221-7945, extension
5442, or by e-mail at MacmillanSpecialMarkets@macmillan.com.

www.fsgbooks.com
www.twitter.com/fsgbooks
www.facebook.com/fsgbooks

1 3 5 7 9 10 8 6 4 2

TO MY DAUGHTERS AND GRANDDAUGHTER:

KIMBERLY, SHOSHANA, AND **IMANI**

CONTENTS

FROM

THE CHAMELEON COUCH

MOJO SONGS

(NEW POEMS)

Say licked clean at birth. Say
    weeping in the tall grass, where
        this tantalizing song begins,
    birds paused on a crooked branch
over a grave of an unending trek
    into the valley of cooling waters.
        Lessons of earth, old questions
    unmoor the first tongue. Say
I have gone back, says the oracle,
    counting seasons & centuries, undoing fault
        lines between one generation & next,
    as she twirls sackcloth edged with pollen,
& one glimpses what one did not know. Say
    this is where the goat was asked to speak
        legends ago, to kneel & deliver a sacrifice.
    To feel a truth depends on how & why
the singer's song fits into the mouth.
    Well, I believe the borrowed-rib
        story is the other way round, entangled
    in decree, blessing, law, & myth. One
only has to listen to nightlong pleas
    of a mother who used all thousand
        chants & prayers of clay, red ocher
    blown from the mouth upon the high
stone wall, retracing a final land bridge

to wishbone. My own two daughters
       & granddaughter, the three know how
   to work praise & lament, ready to sprout
wings of naked flight & labor. Yes,
    hinged into earth, we rose from Lucy
       to clan, from clan to tribe, & today
   we worship her sun-polished bones,
remembering she is made of questions.
    No, mama is not always a first word
       before counting eggs in the cowbird's
   nest. It begins in memory. Now, say
her name, say Dinknesh, mother of us all.

We piled planks, sheets of tin,
& sandbags across the creek
till the bright water rose
& splayed both sides,

swelling into our hoorah.
Our hard work brought July
thrashers & fat June bugs
in decades of dead leaves.

Water moccasins hid in holes
at the brim of the clay bank
as the creek eased up pelvic
bones, hips, navel, & chest,

to eyelevel. When the boys
dove into our swim hole
we pumped our balled fists
to fire up their rebel yells.

The Jim Crow birds sang
of persimmon & mayhaw
after a 12-gauge shotgun
sounded in the mossy woods.

If we ruled the day an hour
the boys would call girl cousins
& sisters, & they came running
half naked into a white splash,

but we could outrun the sunset
through sage & rabbit tobacco,
born to hide each other's alibis
beneath the drowned sky.

SLINGSHOT

A boy's bicycle inner tube
red as inside the body,
a well-chosen forked limb
sawed from a shrub oak,

& then an hour-long squint
to get it right. The taut pull is
everything. There's nothing
without resistance, & the day

holds. The hard, slow, steady
honing flips a beetle on its back,
but the boy refuses to squash it.
He continues with his work.

Summer rambles into a quiet
quantum of dogwood & gum—
a girl he's too shy to tell his name
stands in damp light nearing dark,

& biting a corner of his lip
he whittles the true stock,
knowing wrong from right.
Though Pythagoras owned

a single truth, the boy
untangles a triangle of pull
within a triangle of release,
the slingshot's tongue a tongue

torn out of an old army boot,
& Lord, what a perfect fit.
Feet spread apart, the boy
straddles an imaginary line,

settling quietly into himself
as the balance & pull travel
down through his fingers,
forearm, elbow, into muscle,

up through his shoulder blades,
neck, mouth, set of the jaw,
into the register of the brain,
saying, Take a breath & exhale

slowly, then let the stone fly
as if it has swallowed a stone,
& that is when the boy knows
his body is a compass, a cross.

Bless the woman, man, & child
    who honor earth by opening shine
inside the soil—the splayed hour
    between dampness & dust—to plant
seedlings in double furrows, & then pray
    for cooling rain. Bless the fields,
the catch, the hunt, & the wild fruit,
    & let no one go hungry tonight
or tomorrow. Let the wind & birds
    seed a future ferried into villages
& towns the other side of mountains
    along nameless rivers. Bless those
born with hands made to grapple
    hewn timbers & stone raised from earth
& shaped in circles, who know the geometry
    of corners, & please level the foundation
& pitch a roof so good work isn't diminished
    by rain. Bless the farmer with clouds
in his head, who lugs baskets of dung
    so termites can carve their hives
that hold water long after a downpour
    has gone across the desert & seeds
sprout into a contiguous greening.
    Bless the iridescent beetle working

to haul the heavens down, to journey
　　　from red moondust to excrement.
The wage slave two-steps from Dickens's
　　　tenements among a den of thieves,
blind soothsayers who know shambles
　　　where migrants feathered the nests
of straw bosses as the stonecutters
　　　perfect profiles of robber barons
in granite & marble in town squares
　　　along highways paved for Hollywood.
Bless souls laboring in sweatshops,
　　　& each calabash dipper of water,
the major & minor litanies & ganglia
　　　dangling from promises at the mouth
of the cave, the catcher of vipers at dawn
　　　in the canebrake & flowering fields,
not for love of money but for bread
　　　& clabber on a thick gray slab table,
for the simple blessings in a hamlet
　　　of the storytellers drunk on grog.
Bless the cobbler, molding leather
　　　on his oaken lasts, kneading softness
& give into a red shoe & a work boot,
　　　never giving more to one than the other,
& also the weaver with closed eyes
　　　whose fingers play the ties & loops
as if nothing else matters, daybreak
　　　to sunset, as gritty stories of a people
grow into an epic stitched down
　　　through the ages, the outsider artists

going from twine & hue, cut & tag,
    an ironmonger's credo of steam rising
from buckets & metal dust, & the clang
    of a hammer against an anvil,
& the ragtag ones, a whole motley crew
    at the end of the line, singing ballads
& keeping time on a battered tin drum.

All the little doors unlock
in the brain as the saxophone
nudges the organ & trap drums
till an echo of the Great Migration
tiptoes up & down the bass line.

Faces in semi-dark cluster around
a solo, edging toward a town of steel
& car lines driven by conveyor belts.
But now only a sign stutters across
the Delaware, saying, *Trenton Makes*

The World Takes. With one eye
on the players at the Candlelight
& the other on televised Olympians
home is a Saturday afternoon
around the kidney-shaped bar.

These songs run along dirt roads
& highways, crisscross lonely seas
& scale mountains, traverse skies
& underworlds of neon honkytonk,
wherever blues dare to travel.

A swimmer climbs a diving board
in Beijing, does a springy toe dance
on the edge, turns her head
toward us, & seems to say, Okay,
you guys, now see if you can play this.

She executes a backflip,
a triple spin, a half twist,
held between now & then,
& jackknifes through the water,
& it is what pours out of the horn.

Becky grew up in the provinces of the blackest, richest Delta silt this side of cut & run. When the wind rampaged in from the east she could taste the soil, & naturally it was biblical. The boy came one June morning to work on her daddy's egg farm. Both were fourteen—he three days older than she. His job was to feed the two-thousand-odd white leghorn hens, to gather the pearly ovals in baskets & carry them to the grading shed where Stella cleaned off flecks of shit & held each egg up to a beaming light, then placed them into white dozen-size papery cartons. Sometimes Becky worked beside the tall black woman for the fun of it, mirroring her moves. Also, she liked looking at the boy gathering the eggs. But they didn't dare let anyone else see their catlike eyes. In their four years of stolen kisses they grew into each other. They'd lie in the tall grass, trembling in an embrace. But one day the boy enlisted in the army. Stella would say, "Miz Becky, I know a lady who can take that spell off ya." Of course, Becky would say, "I don't know what you talkin 'bout, Stella." A year later, Becky married Buster Collins from across the river. The couple built a nice brick bungalow two miles down the road. She kept saying, "Buster, I wanna baby." Three years passed. The boy came back. He began driving a tractor & trailer across country. To this day Becky can't say why she slipped Stella the note to give him. *When the setting sun lights the door of the hayloft.* The two began to meet. It didn't make sense, they both declared. But one night they caught themselves in the bedroom while Buster sat in the living room watching championship wrestling, drinking his bottles of Dixie. The boy almost called Buster's name. He whispered to Becky, "Never again." She pounded her fists against his chest, saying, "Over my dead body." That was the night she ran from the bedroom crying. That was the night she told the sheriff the window was open but she only heard bullfrogs in the gully before she felt his knife at her throat. She didn't holler because she saw murder in his eyes. When the sheriff & his two deputies stopped the truck at the state line, the sheriff said, "Boys, looka here, a dead nigger drivin a big fancy rig to hell." He didn't try telling them his side of the story. If he had, they would've killed him on the spot. Mayflies clogged the air. They dragged him bloody into a jail cell. A hoot owl called. Just before daybreak the mob appeared. The sheriff handed over the keys. Years later, after what happened, his name was the answer to an unspeakable divination. It had something to do with a tin coffee can of charred bones & ashes in a shoebox of dried rose petals. Becky said there are legends that eat graveyard clay, though she never could wrap her mind 'round that one. She caught a sundown Greyhound headed north & thought of Stella's drinking gourd. Its orangey-gold hue. Now, she sits on a midnight curb in a ghetto, beckoning to whatever danger walks near, still trying to decide what Billie Joe McAllister & that girl tossed off the Tallahatchie Bridge. Was it life or death? Or some damnable other something, a heavy lodestone? Becky always had an imagination to die for. Hadn't that song showed her feet the highway? Now, after all these years, all the other stories were balled up in hers. She gazes up crook-eyed at the sky, a Delta sunset tamped down into her bones, & now a limp easing into her left leg.

The hard work of love sealed
in language has stolen me far
from home, from the fields,
& I see morning mist rising
where they borrow ghosts
to get even with each other,
harvesting vegetable & fruit
close as we can get to dirt.
I glimpse shadows smudged
in trees lining the highway
where night & day commingle,
or as a season moves this slow hour,
saying, Bad things happened here.
At first, the figures seem to be
staring into earth, like migrants
who work Florida & California,
unearthing what we live to eat.

We know the men from women
by the colors they wear, sweat
ringing their lives in gray shade,
& our bus makes the mushroom
gatherers with pails & canvas bags
blur among the trees as if shutters
are opening & closing, as the mind

runs to keep up. But the road forks
here in eastern Europe, & I hardly
can see faces in the door of leaves.
The women know where to stand
in the clearing, how each trucker
slows down to make the curve,
& cannot miss yellow or purple.
He honks his loud bluesy horn,
idling at the bottom of the hill
on a thin shoulder of blacktop.

The battle begins here as I slap my chest
with the palm of my hand, a talking drum
under the skin. It's hard to believe men
once marched into fire blowing bagpipes
& fifes. Thunder & lightning can disarm us
like IEDs & RPGs. We say to ourselves,
Keep a cool head, & don't forget the pass
& review. Salute the dead but don't linger.
The rank & file are you & I. But mother of
courage knows the weight of ammo belts,
to zigzag across dunes & around acacias,
& to never forget the smell of a burn pit.
Draw down faces of battle on a sketch pad.
But the pigment of ink-jets will never be
blood & skin worked into an anthem.
The drawings dare us to step closer, to look
into our eyes reflected in the glass, framed
by the camera's automatic mind. To follow
songs of the Highwaymen is one way not
to fight oneself in a parade of mirrors.
To lie down in a desert & not think war,
white grains on the skin. To question
is to be human. To interrogate shadows
or go into terrain & unweave the map.

To lag over the small moments ferries us
across rivers. To stand naked before a mirror
& count the parts is to question the whole
season of sowing & reaping thorns.

THE MOUNTAIN

In the hard, unwavering mountain
light, black flags huddle at the foot of the mountain.

Hours are days & nights, a ragged map
of hungry faces trapped on the mountain.

But silence swears help is on its way,
formations rolling toward the mountain.

Blood of the sacred yew & stud goat
beg repose midpoint of the mountain

& prayers rise in August's predawn gruff.
Artillery halts at the foot of the mountain.

Help is on its way, but don't question
the music burning toward the mountain.

Infidels size up their easy targets, flying
skull & bone as villainy scales the mountain.

It could be a beautiful day but black flags
throng around the base of the mountain.

The red-wing kite has come to pinpoint
a medieval hour, circling the mountain.

Men, women, & children change rags of rebirth
lost in the double shadow of the mountain,

& a ghost of gunmetal drones overhead
& slowly turns, translating the mountain,

then stops midair, before drumming down
the black flags at the foot of the mountain.

They work fingers to bone, & borrow
smudged paper, then make promises
to family, unmerciful gods, the unborn.
Some eat a favorite meal three times
in a row. Others partake only a pinch
of soil before boarding half-broken boats
& rubber rafts—half of the young women
big with life inside them, flesh & blood
for daydreams of the Arabian nights,
as makeshift charts & constellations
work their way through war & rumors
of war. The smugglers count their loot.
Hard winds rattle gongs over sea salt
till the rusty engines die, & their cries
moonstruck sirens, pirated schooners
adrift under a mute sky, rock to & fro,
& the fight goes out of the few alive.
Their relatives & friends, old lost folk
songs, mountains & valleys, all left
behind. Searchlights spot the dead
hugging the living. Draglines raise them.
Pray for those who're braver than us.
The lucky ones stumble out of stupor,
tried by raging water in morning light,
enchanted by lingo of the albatross.

When they call him Old School
he clears his throat, squares
his shoulders, & looks straight
into their unlit eyes, saying,
"I was born by the damn river
& I've been running ever since."
An echo of Sam Cooke hangs
in bruised air, & for a minute

the silence of Fate reigns over
day & night, a tilt of the Earth
body & soul caught in a sway
going back to reed & goatskin,
back to trade winds locked
inside an "Amazing Grace"
which will never again sound
the same after Charleston,

South Carolina, & yes, words
follow the river through pine
& oak, muscadine & redbud,
& the extinct Lord God bird
found in an inventory of green
shadows longing for the scent
of woe & beatitude, taking root
in the mossy air of some bayou.

Now Old School can't stop
going from a sad yes to gold,
into a season's bloomy creed,
& soon he only hears Martha
& the Vandellas, their dancing
in the streets, through a before
& after. Mississippi John Hurt,
Ma Rainey, Sleepy John Estes,

Son House, Skip James, Joe
Turner, & Sweet Emma,
& he goes till what he feels
wears out his work boots
along the sidewalks, his life
a fist of coins in a coat pocket
to give to the recent homeless
up & down these city blocks.

He knows "We Shall Overcome"
& anthems of the flower children
which came after Sister Rosetta,
Big Mama Thornton, & Bo Diddley.
Now, the years add up to a sharp
pain in his left side on Broadway,
but the Five Blind Boys of Alabama
call down an evening mist to soothe.

He believes to harmonize is
to reach, to ascend, to query
ego & hold a note till there's

only a quiver of blue feathers
at dawn, & a voice goes out
to return as a litany of mock
orange & sweat, as we are sewn
into what we came crying out of,

& when Old School declares,
"You can't doo-wop a cappella
& let your tongue touch an evil
while fingering a slothful doubt
beside the Church of Coltrane,"
he has traversed the lion's den
as Eric Dolphy plays a fluted
solo of birds in the peppertrees.

THE BODY REMEMBERS

I stood on one foot for three minutes & didn't tilt
the scales. Do you remember how quickly

we scrambled up an oak leaning out over the creek,
how easy to trust the water to break

our glorious leaps? The body remembers
every wish one lives for or doesn't, or even horror.

Our dance was a rally in sunny leaves, then quick
as anything, Johnny Dickson was up opening

his wide arms in the tallest oak, waving
to the sky, & in the flick of an eye

he was a buffalo fish gigged, pleading
for help, voiceless. Bigger & stronger,

he knew every turn in the creek past his back door,
but now he was cooing like a brown dove

in a trap of twigs. A water-honed spear
of kindling jutted up, as if it were the point

of our folly & humbug on a Sunday afternoon, right?
Five of us carried him home through the thicket,

our feet cutting a new path, running in sleep
years later. We were young as condom-balloons

flowering crab apple trees in double bloom
& had a world of baleful hope & breath.

Does Johnny run fingers over the thick welt
on his belly, days we were still invincible?

Sometimes I spend half a day feeling for bones,
humming a half-forgotten ballad

on a park bench a long ways from home.
The body remembers the berry bushes

heavy with sweetness shivering in a lonely woods,
but I doubt it knows words live longer

than clay & spit of flesh, as rock-bottom love.
Is it easier to remember pleasure

or does hurt ease truest hunger?
Our summer, rocking back & forth, uprooting

what's to come, the shadow of the tree
weighed as much as a man.

TALKING DIRTY

TO THE GODS

HOMO ERECTUS

After pissing around his gut-level
Kingdom, he builds a fire & hugs
A totem against his chest.
Cheetahs pace the horizon

To silence a grassy cosmos
Where carrion birds sing
Darkness back from the hills.
Something in the air, quintessence or rancor,

Makes a langur bash the skull
Of another male's progeny.
The mother tries to fight him off,
But this choreographer for Jacob

& the Angel knows defeat
Arrives in an old slam dance
& applied leverage—the Evening Star
In both eyes, something less than grace.

UTETHEISA ORNATRIX, THE FIRST GODDESS

Mottled with eyes, she's a snag
Of silk from a blood orange
Kimono. This moth, a proto-
Goddess, flits about as if grafted

To an uneasy moment. A little machine
Inside, she coaxes every male to deposit
Sperm, & weighs each with an unholy
Exactitude. She can correct

A mistake with metabolic
Absolution. Only the biggest is
Fertilized, & all the others grow
Into nutrients for her. Food

Defines them. Otherwise,
They depend on promiscuous
Wings to beat till their world
Turns into light & sap.

NIGHT RITUAL

The spotted hyena
Dances, her mock penis
Aimed at the moon. A mile away
A king cobra flares its hood

& strikes a lion. He kneels
Under a pendulous firmament as the venom
Takes hold. She's graceful, nimbused,
Leading her quarrelsome legion. Eyes

Flicker like stars along the timberline,
Yellow lights through grass,
& Botswana turns under their single-minded
Creed. They try to outrun luscious

Blood, till they're a tussle
Of moonlight. She's the first to sink
Teeth into the lion's belly, & yanks
With all the strength gods entrusted to her.

LIME

The victorious army marches into the city,
& not far behind tarries a throng of women
Who slept with the enemy on the edge
Of battlements. The stunned morning

Opens into a dust cloud of hooves
& drums. Some new priests cradle
Stone tablets, & others are poised
With raised mallets in a forest of defeated

Statuary. Of course, behind them
Linger the turncoats & pious
Merchants of lime. What's Greek
Is forged into Roman; what's Roman

Is hammered into a ceremony of birds
Headed east. Whatever is marble
Burns in the lime kilns because
Someone dreams of a domed bathhouse.

ODE TO THE MAGGOT

Brother of the blowfly
& godhead, you work magic
Over battlefields,
In slabs of bad pork

& flophouses. Yes, you
Go to the root of all things.
You are sound & mathematical.
Jesus Christ, you're merciless

With the truth. Ontological & lustrous,
You cast spells on beggars & kings
Behind the stone door of Caesar's tomb
Or split trench in a field of ragweed.

No decree or creed can outlaw you
As you take every living thing apart. Little
Master of earth, no one gets to heaven
Without going through you first.

They're here. Among blades
Of grass, like divided cells.
Between plant & animal. Good
For nothing. In a rainstorm, spores

Glom together. Yellow-white
Pieces of a puzzle. Unable to be
Seen till united. Something
Left over from a world before—

Beyond modern reason. Primeval
Fingers reduced & multiplied
A hundredfold, the most basic
Love & need shaped them into a belief

System. The color of scrambled eggs.
Good for something we never thought
About, these pets of aliens crawl up
The Judas trees in bloom.

SLOTH

If you're one of seven
Downfalls, up in your kingdom
Of mulberry leaves, there are men
Betting you aren't worth a bullet,

That your skin won't tan into a good
Wallet. As if drugged in the womb
& limboed in a honeyed languor,
By the time you open your eyes

A thousand species have lived
& died. Born on a Sunday
Morning, with old-world algae
In your long hair, a goodness

Disguised your two-toed claws
Bright as flensing knives. In this
Upside-down haven, you're reincarnated
As a fallen angel trying to go home.

NIPPLES

As if my mind's double-jointed
Sometimes, I have wanted
To bow my head & kiss
My sad, stingy nipples.

I have desired music to live
Beneath the skin, with the same
Hairless ease & untamed yearning
As the *Kritios Boy* who outwitted

Time's polish. I am bowed
To questions in my head before
I was born. Hungry to kiss jubilation
Into my body, I can almost remember

When I was a girl. After the breaking
& breaking in, now these nubbins
& nips are purely aesthetic, two
Abbreviated peepholes.

SCAPEGOAT

The alpha wolf chooses his mate
For life, & the other she-wolves
Stare at the ground. Yellowish
Light drains from notorious eyes

Of the males, stealing their first
& last sex. The pack's outcast,
The albino we humans love,
Whimpers, wags his tail,

& crawls forward on his belly.
He never sleeps at night.
After pacing down thorny grass
Where the alpha male urinated,

A shadow limps off among the trees.
Already sentenced into wilderness,
As if born wounded, he must stand
Between man & what shines.

VENUS OF WILLENDORF

She's big as a man's fist,
Big as a black-pepper shaker
Filled with gris-gris dust,
Like two fat gladiolus bulbs

Grown into a burst of twilight.
Lumpy & fertile, earthy
& egg-shaped, she's pregnant
With all the bloomy hosannas

Of love hunger. Beautiful
In a way that forces us to look
At the ground, this squat
Venus in her braided helmet

Is carved from a hunk of limestone
Shaped into a blues singer.
In her big smallness
She makes us kneel.

SLAVES AMONG BLADES OF GRASS

The Amazon ants dispatch
Scouts armed with mandibles
Sharp as sabers. They return
To drum each other's heads

With antennae, & then send out
Columns of warriors to surround a nest
& abduct pupae. As if made for battle,
With jaws so deadly they can't feed

Themselves, they possess slaves.
New blades of grass beaded with water
Light a subkingdom beneath
Shadowed footsteps where the sky

Meets indiscernible green of river
& jungle, in this terrain
Where a world is dismantled
To make something else look whole.

When the grand master of folly
Turns to see if other mortals
Are looking at him & Hermaphrodite,
A hairline crack runs beneath

The Pompeian fresco, & we feel
Like children at a Saturday matinee
On the verge of shouting *Don't*
Across the river Acheron.

We see Hermaphrodite's muscle
Beneath the rounded whiteness,
& already know the outcome of this
Tussle of light & panic against

Disrobed stone. We're there
With them, where one is another,
On the precipice of Hesiod's field
As the wind sings false things true.

SEX TOYS

Lined up like toy soldiers
In the attitude of pillage,
They're filled with nothing but ohs
& ahs. One endless night, a tool

Of torture, & next day, a godsend
Illustration of the pleasure principle
Molded or carved into pliable mystery
& elation. Prometheus said the king of Albe

Wanted his daughter to couple with a phallus
Which appeared in his chimney, but she sent
A servant who became the mother of Romulus
& Remus. Made of aluminum or hard rubber,

As if we need something to help
Break hearts & leave slow nicks
In stony soil, these instruments
Raise temples beneath reason & skin.

This can make hard men
Confess to how much water
They're made of: the saliva
It takes to polish river stones

Into a levee song. Which godhead
Did someone steal this blueprint
From in a dream? The blind prisoner
Who refused to draw a circle in dust

Around his executioner, he knew
What the Latin verb *pollere* meant
To the Greeks who said *anticheir*
(Another hand). But that was before

Ovid used the gods as punch lines,
When they were still in the trees
& hadn't yet climbed down
To curse the human thumb.

BEDAZZLED

A jeweled wasp stuns
A cockroach & plants an egg
Inside. In no time, easy
As fear eats into someone,

The translucent larva grows
Beneath its host's burnished
Shell. The premature stinger
Waits like a bad idea, almost

Hidden. Summertime
Breathes on a thorny leaf.
Before the new wasp breaks
Free, they are one. No longer

Fat on death's fugacity,
By tomorrow afternoon
It will cling to a window screen
Bright as Satan's lost tiepin.

THE CONGO SNAKE

Feet of petty chances, you
Came out on the other side
Of love & mercy. No one
Cares if you rise from the lower world

Or not, as something to grind up
For cat food, & even the hunger
Of gods can't wish you away.
In your cave of primordial mud,

Window through slow water,
We pray only ghosts & goblins
Look at you. The untouchables
Tattoo your image on the soles

Of their feet. The monkey
God swears you don't exist,
& in the house of good tidings
The devil is blessed before you.

THE LURE

The batfish hides there
At the bottom of desire.
A fleshy, wormlike lure
Dangles freely, luminescent

As a French tickler or line
From a love song personified.
Without eyes or guts, the male
Grows into the female, a Jonah

Inside a scaled-down Moby Dick.
She's bewitched among sea hair
& kelp, filled with forbearance
& a silent singing bitten in half,

In a holy world of mouths
Speaking watery reprieves
In needful hush, down where
His first breath was an open wound.

INFIDELITY

Zeus always introduces himself
As one who needs stitching
Back together with kisses.
Like a rock star in leather

& sapphires—conflagration
& a trick of silk falling
Between lost chances & never
Again. His disguises are almost

Mathematical, as Io & Europa
Pass from their dreams into his.
This lord of storm clouds
Is also a sun god crooning desire

& dalliance in a garden of nymphs.
Some days, he loves gloxinia,
& others, craves garlic blooms—
Hera, Aegina, & Callisto in the same song.

UKIYO-E

We turn away from the flesh
On paper, but find ourselves
Praising the flow of feudal silk
& rice powder, as a samurai's gaze

Unfastens a windfall of blossoms
In some house of assignation
The other side of Hiroshige's forecast
Of slanted black rain. Somehow,

We face Utamaro's hairy ape
Who brandishes his penis
Like an untutored sword
At a pale maiden against indigo.

The two are brushed into a tussle
Of fire with water, a fury of silk
In a floating world, a season
Of flowered branches breaking.

AMBER

The eyedropper of holy water
Didn't do the job. Night & day
He's been hunched over his microscope
After tweezering the extinct beetle

From resin. Holding up the tube
To glassy light that weighs less
Than fear, he knows a sneeze could destroy
His work. He's sure the millennial wings

Would blink open & stir
If he could find a half teaspoon
Of birth water. He can almost see
The hand that wore the Etruscan

Ring. Beneath the magnified glow
A touch of anger illuminates
A shadow. He tilts it right
& left, & the beetle swells.

ODE TO DUST

It speaks when the anonymous
Tongue of each feather & leaf
Quivers, swearing that nothing's changed
As we touch tables & lampshades.

We breathe it in as if something
Is always beginning beneath the ruins
& perennials, mending skin under
The surface. Even the slow patina

Of the quietest lesson takes hold
Of Gudea's *Architectural Plans*,
Working while we sleep.
As if conjured by regret,

It lives on the imagination
Of all-night ghosts, like the worm
Brought forth from the feminine
Temples of wood & apple.

BODY OF A WOMAN
(CADAVERE DI DONNA)

Here you are, still
Reposed behind glass
Like a work of art. Yes,
Body of precious aloneness,

There are times I desire you
In a lover's arms. Sometimes
I want you making fierce love,
With moans like thought bubbles

Of pleasure forever in Pompeii's
Lava & ash. Yet, other nights,
As Miles Davis plays ballads
In the background, like tonight,

There's only irony: I see
You're gazing out toward
The House of the Faun,
Waiting for someone.

REMUS & ROMULUS

They're at the eight teats
Of the Capitoline she-wolf,
Their naked adoration
Suspended in a leap

Of faith. Is she stone
Or bronze? If we lie
To ourselves long enough,
Practice works underneath

The pattern of this heft
Till flesh finds a way to rise
To a level of blame. The boys
Face each other, & we can see

Brutus's plot in the wolf's
Vulnerability, in her tarnished
Stare. Now she's only primal food
& sex, their first coup d'état.

PAN

Elizabeth, I must say,
Pan wasn't raising Cain among the reeds.
He had taken off his mask,
& was lying there, puffing ganja,

Blowing Rasta smoke rings
& nibbling on a golden mango,
When he glimpsed three naiads
Prancing beside the lily pond.

He rolled over & watched two ants
Struggle up a Sisyphean incline
With a moth. Silenus's brother
& father, scapegoat & earthly god,

He felt divided. The nymphs frolicked
As he played love & panic on his flute
Till Arcady drifted out of his head,
& then a whisper opened all the buds.

EPITHALAMIUM

We washed away the live perfume
Of others, removed lush memories
Of their hands, trying to ignore kisses
Burning in our mouths, songs

Left in the inner ear, next
To a flowering bone. The hills
Climbed in the midnight blue distance
Were each other. Paths, detours,

& inclines dazzled us with mirages,
Chanced escapes. The city's roughhousing
Light-years away; no amount of blood red
Sirens could tear us apart,

Not till the blissful damage
Began to heal. Our beasts, a lion
& bull, slept side by side, as if born
To remove the other's curse.

I don't know, can't say when they first
Shook hips like rock stars
& uprooted. Maybe they stole
Flight from Nike of Samothrace

& the altar of Zeus at Pergamum,
Or modeled after the winged god
On a silver coin from Peparethus.
Do you think an angel is nothing

But an idea grafted to a shadow
As monsters sprout from foreheads,
Feathered to muffle sacred blows?
I don't remember weighing a stone

With a blackbird's broken wing,
But I know when the question flew
Into my head I was standing here
At the kitchen window drying dishes.

EROS

He's on a hammock in Bangkok,
Eating succulent prawns & squid
Spiced with red pepper & lemongrass.
Hesiod's "Fairest of the deathless

Gods" can feel the fatigue syndrome
Loosen its grip in this archipelago
Of pleasures. He reads a pirated
Edition of *The Plague*. At twilight,

He'll go to the corner shop
& buy a jade brooch for Muriel
Back in Boise. He'll return
To Club Limbo. A new counterfeit

Gift dipped in fire. Eros throws
A kiss to the teenage prostitute,
& touches the wad of greenbacks
Nestled against his groin.

The maypole glistens with pig fat.
Thousands of mayflies (I call them
Lovebugs) died the first hours
Against windshields, headlights,

Hoods, or sucked into the grillwork's
Wide grin. In humid dusk,
A sheet of sex hangs & bulbous bees
Nudge mayflowers till pain runs

Into pleasure. A bounty of failures
Swells with timorous maydew & mayblob,
As if something is loved beyond mercy.
Maybirds frolic in shambles of dawn

& ignite mayweed. Sweetheart,
Can I, may I? Should I stop
Undoing these seven bone-colored
Buttons too pretty to look at?

LUST

If only he could touch her,
Her name like an old wish
In the stopped weather of salt
On a snail. He longs to be

Words, juicy as passion fruit
On her tongue. He'd do anything,
Dance three days & nights
To make the most terrible gods

Rise out of ashes of the yew,
To step from the naked
Fray, to be as tender
As meat imagined off

The bluegill's pearlish
Bones. He longs to be
An orange, to feel fingernails
Run a seam through him.

I want Catullus
In every line, a barb
The sun plays for good
Luck. I need to know if iron

Tastes like laudanum
Or a woman. I already sense
What sleeps in the same flesh,
Ariadne & her half brother

Caught in the other's dream.
I want each question to fit me
Like a shiny hook, a lure
In the gullet. What it is

To look & know how much muscle
It takes to lift a green slab.
I need a Son House blues
To wear out my tongue.

SHIVA

He wandered nude out of Eden
Smiling at spellbound women in trees
& doorways. A breeze shook
Incense from leaves. They tore off

Their clothes, blocked his path,
& fell in the writhing dust.
They never knew so many kisses
Were stored inside their bodies.

His thick hair smelled of cedar.
He'd once worn a garland of skulls,
Dusted himself with funeral ashes,
& stood beside a river. A sacred tree,

Dark-skinned, almost African, *Supreme
Lord* in person. The wives followed
This beggar with the erect penis,
A trembling left in the lilies.

A SMALL SYSTEM

The Galápagos finch
Clutches a cactus thorn
In her beak. She works
Fast as a fencing master,

& we can almost see the brain
Grow. In a sky of orchids
Below, she spots a viper
Tonguing petals—the first

Desire. Once, what the worm
Taught us was sacred,
Serene as the beetle
Grub the bird now jabs

With her spear. Finely tuned
As a red-capped woodpecker,
She prances like God's little
Torquemada on the highest rotten branch.

HOMUNCULUS

Van Gogh's sunflowers blot out
My sky, while each cat's-eye burns
A vigil. The chief alchemist
Squeezes a dropper of love

To jump-start my heart. A voice so small
Only the watchdog hears my magnanimous
Prayer to carved intaglios. Outside
This chemical window, salamanders

& geckos are monsters. A mosquito hawk
Magnifies into a hang glider.
A honey-locust thorn
Sir Lancelot's javelin.

My ego, if crystallized, would fit
Into the eye socket of a hummingbird.
I may be less than your last thought, but,
Look, here's my thimble of gin.

ECSTATIC

Joy, use me like a whore.
Turn me inside out like Donne
Desired God to do with him.
Show me some muscle,

Sunlight on black stone.
Coldcock me about the head
Till I moan like a bell, low
As the one Goya could hear

Through the walls of
Quinta del Sordo.
Tie me up to the stocks those Puritans
Handled so well in Boston streets.

Don't let me down. I beg
You to use all your know-how
In one throttle. Please, good God,
Put everything into your swing.

SPEED BALL

Didn't Chet Baker know
They'd make a great white hope
Jump hoops of fire on the edge
Of midnight gigs that never happened?

Miles hipped him at the Lighthouse
About horse, said not to feel guilty
About *DownBeat* in '53. Chet stole
Gasoline to sniff, doctored with Beiderbecke's

Chicago style. But it wasn't long
Before he was a toothless lion
Gazing up at his face like a stranger's
Caught by tinted lens & brass. Steel

Blue stare from Oklahoma whispering for
"A kind of high that scares everyone
To death." Maybe a bop angel, Slim
Greer, pulled him from that hotel window.

A FAMOUS GHOST

I thought happiness my birthright
& married the bone structure
In Mother's dreams, his English
Impeccable. Though they sift

My ashes & swear I fought
The shadows of his lovers,
I am not Propertius's Cynthia.
Where I stand, it is still '63

& the flags are at half-mast.
I never wanted to be famous,
But couldn't lift my head off
The oven door. My last breath

Stole from his. Fumes slipped
Down like a prayer to the Cubist
In the basement. No, I'm not Hostia,
Though I unlaced a corset of stardust.

AVARICE

At six, she chewed off
The seven porcelain buttons
From her sister's christening gown
& hid them in a Prince Albert can

On a sill crisscrossing the house
In the spidery crawl space.
She'd weigh a peach in her hands
Till it rotted. At sixteen,

She gazed at her little brother's
June bugs pinned to a sheet of cork.
Assaying their glimmer, till she
Buried them beneath a fig tree's wide,

Green skirt. Now, twenty-six,
Locked in the beauty of her bones,
She counts eight engagement rings
At least twelve times each day.

ROLLERBLADES

Knucklehead spins on a wish & lucky
Star, dividing the city into hellbent
Circles, one improvisation to the next
Double-or-nothing dare. He grabs the bumper

Of a yellow cab & traverses Central Park,
Skirring & looping through rings, plugged
Into the Delfonics & Beastie Boys.
Zip, skid, & bone spindle . . .

Knucklehead hangs inside the bottom half
Of Odysseus's dreamt map to a country
Of lotus-eaters, e-mail, & goof-off.
Hugging curves beside the thieves of his image,

He ducks into a labyrinth of close
Calls. Their eyes collide. Knucklehead
Pivots, as if the four wheels of each blade
Could guillotine an apparition's last effigy.

MONKEY WRENCH

Balled into a cocked fist, sure
As a hammerlock, the pipe's cracked sleeve
Is sealed in corrosion. Elbow
Grease, leverage, anger, & oil,

Nothing works. The vise grip
Opens an icy mouth, dribbling
Rusty sighs. I almost give up, before
I see the wrench propped near a blowtorch

Beside the washing machine, inside my head
Like an abused blessing, awaiting the promise
& caress of an oily rag. I lie on my back
Beneath the house, among broken Nehi bottles,

Dog hair, & insect wings, as if the forces
Have been hard at work on a piecemeal angel.
Full of Christmas cake & eggnog, I squint up
At clandestine eyes in a loom of spiderwebs.

I weigh you, a minute in each hand,
With the sun & a woman's perfume
In my senses, a need to smooth
Everything down. You belong

To a dead man, made to fit
A keyhole of metal to search
For light, to rasp burrs off
In slivers thin as hair, true

Only to slanted grooves cut
Across your tempered spine.
I'd laugh when my father said
Rat-tail. Now, slim as hope

& solid as remorse
In your red mausoleum,
Whenever I touch you
I crave something hard.

THE GOD OF LAND MINES

He sits on a royal purple cushion
Like a titanic egg. Dogs whimper
& drag themselves on all fours through dirt
When a breeze stirs his sweet perfume.

He looks like a legless, armless
Humpty-Dumpty, & if someone waves
A photo of an amputee outside the Imperial
Palace in Hue, he'd never blink.

When he thinks *doors*, they swing open.
When dust gushes on the horizon
His face is a mouthless smile.
He can't stop loving steel.

He's oblong & smooth as a watermelon.
The contracts arrive already signed.
Lately, he feels like seeds in a jar,
Swollen with something missing.

Maybe he thought gods
Would gaze back through these eyeholes
Of leather soft as Leda,
Smoother than vellum.

He said, "Life, here's Death
With his orphic grin."
In the glass case is Mirth,
Over here Metamorphosis.

This is Quintus Roselus.
He called it "Beauty
Turned inside out
By what is seen."

Here's my favorite, *The Plastic
Bag*. Look how one mask fits
Inside another, how they kiss
Away each other's fear.

POSTSCRIPT TO A SUMMER NIGHT

As if he'd stood too long facing
A pharaoh in the Temple of Karnak
Or Hermes of Siphnos, one night
J. R. Midas copied his penis

On the company's Xerox machine,
Lying across a bed of hot light.
He was thirty-three, still half
Invincible, & scribbled on each: *I am*

On fire with love, & all the more fire
Because I am rejected . . . He x-ed out
Galatea, & wrote in names of the two
New district managers: *Melissa, Amy*

Lou. He hung his coat & tie on a hook,
Then strolled down to the docks
& walked under an orange moon
Till his clothes turned to rags.

Today, somewhere, a man
In his early seventies is lost
In a cluster of hills at dusk,
Kneeling beside a huckleberry bush.

It's been six—no, seven—days
Since he stood at his kitchen window
Gazing out toward this summit
As Armstrong's "Gully Low Blues"

Played on his Philco, hoping
The hot brass would undercut
The couple's techno & punk rock
In the basement. Two days ago,

He ate the last trail mix & beef
Jerky. Now, with a blues note in his head,
He nuzzles the berried branches
To his mouth, like a young deer.

CURANDERISMO

Dear, I roll this duck egg
Over your breasts to steal
The poison, old troubles,
& lamentation. The angry cells

Will sprout in this sacrifice
That now takes on your burdens
& pleas. The mystery of gods
Lives on our bodies. I want you

To take this icon, my dear,
Wrap it in a silk garment,
& bury it thirty-three paces
Among the trees. Disbelief

Can't change what's happened here
Tonight, with these bad omens
Zonked, & I can't think ugly
Since I deal in cosmic stuff.

THE POLECAT

Thanks for your warning
Along the chilly hedgerow.
I have seen dogs roll in the dust
& run in circles, nudge the hemlock,

Trying to shake off the essence
Of you. Your scent rises up
Through the living-room floorboards,
The odor of fear from saw vines

& cockleburs. I fold both hands
Into a mask. Those days, in love,
Protesting for the spotted owl
Among my last good witnesses,

I remember a sheriff aiming pepper gas.
Praised or damned, it depends where
We stand, little terrorist
Of the stink bomb.

CROW LINGO

Can you be up to any good
Grouped into a shadow against Venus,
Congregated on power lines around
The edges of cornfields?

Luck. Curse. A wedding.
Death. I have seen you peck
Pomegranates & then cawcawcaw
Till hornets rise from purple flesh

& juice. I know you're plotting
An overthrow of the government
Of sparrows & jays, as the high council
Of golden orioles shiver among maple

& cottonwood. Your language
Of passwords has no songs,
No redemption in wet feathers
Slicked back, a crook's iridescent hair.

The master craftsman sits like Rodin's
Thinker, surrounded by his cosmic tools,
Experimenting with the greenhouse effect
& acid rain. A great uncertainty

Plagues him. Some hard questions
Wound the air. Yesterday afternoon
Children marched with a rainbow
Of placards. Perhaps he can create

A few suicides with his new computer
Virus. Something has gone wrong
In the shop, because the old gods
Of serpentine earthquakes & floods

Are having more fun than he is
In his laboratory of night sweats
& ethnic weapons. Lovers smile
As Cupid loads a blowgun with thorns.

MUD

She works in the corner of the porch
Where a trumpet vine crawls up to falling
Light. There's always some solitary
Bridge to cross. Right hand

& left hand. The dirt dauber
Shapes a divided cell
Out of everything she knows,
Back & forth between the ditch.

I could take a stick & play
God. Soldier. Sadist. Nosing
Mud into place, she hums the world's
Smallest motor. Later, each larva

Quivers like bait on a hook . . . spermatozoa
Clustered in a song of clay. So small
Only the insignificance can begin
To fill the afternoon.

Hands make love to thigh, breast, clavicle,
Willed to each other, to the keyboard—
Searching the whole forest of compromises
Till the soft engine kicks in, running

On honey. Dissonance worked
Into harmony, evenhanded
As Art Tatum's plea to the keys.
Like a woman & man who have lived

A long time together, they know how
To keep the song alive. Wordless
Epics into the cold night, keepers
Of the fire—the right hand lifts

Like the ghost of a sparrow
& the left uses every motionless muscle.
Notes divide, balancing each other,
Love & hate tattooed on the fingers.

TABOO

Herodotus, woven into his story,
    tells how the Phoenicians lent
        war fleets to Greece & Egypt,

how a ghost-driven flotilla
    eased like salmon up birth water
        & sailed the Red Sea,

hoping to circumnavigate Africa
    around the Cape of Good Hope
        & along Gibraltar. A blue

door opened. Diodorus
    says of the Ethiopians,
        "born under the Sun's path,"

that "its warmth may have ripened them
    earlier than other men." As if
        a ventriloquist inherited

the banter of a sailor's parrot,
    words weave with Herodotus's—
        angel food . . . sellers didn't touch

the gold . . . devil's food. The stories
become flesh as these ghosts
argue about what's lost

in translation, believing two images
should spawn & ignite a star
in the eyes of a sphinx

or soothsayer. Sometimes they do.
There's a reason why the dead
may talk through a medium

about how Aryans drove cattle
along the seven rivers & left
dark-skinned Dravidians

with tongues cut out, sugarcane
fields ablaze, & the holy air
smelling of ghee & soma.

These ghosts know the power
of suggestion is more than body
language: white list, black

sheep, white tie, black market.
Fear climbs the tribal brainstem
or wills itself up an apple tree,

hiding from the dream animal
inside. The serpent speaks
like a Lacan signifier,

posing as a born-again agrarian
    who loves computer terminals
        better than cotton blossoms

planted, then we wail to reap
    whirlwind & blessing. Each prefix
        clings like a hookworm

inside us. If not the split-tongued
    rook, the sparrow is condemned
        to sing the angel down.

IMHOTEP

His forehead was stamped, *Administrator*
  of the Great Mansion. Unloved in the
    Crescent City, I sat in a bathtub

clutching a straight razor.
  Desire had sealed my mouth
    with her name. I asked,

What do full moons & secret herbs
  have to do with a man's heartache?
    But this sage from the island of Philae

just smiled. Here before me stood the Son
  of Ptah. Dung beetles & amethyst . . .
    cures for a mooncalf,

flaccidity, bad kidneys, gout,
  & gallstones. What we knew
    about the blood's map

went back to the court
  of King Zoser. Something
    beneath this April dream

scored by voices passing
    outside my front door, a rap song
        thundering from a boogie box.

I wasn't dead. This Homeric healer
    from the Serapeum of Memphis
        lingered in the room.

I folded the bright blade
    back into its mother-of-pearl
        handle, & laughed at the noise

in the street, at a yellow moth
    beating wings into dust
        against a windowpane.

BACCHANAL

Rubens paints desire
    in his wife's eyes
        gazing up at the black man

who has an arm around
    her waist. Tambourines
        shake the dusky air alive,

& there's a hint of tulips,
    a boy touching his penis
        at the edge of jubilation.

Has a war been won, have dogs
    been driven from the gates,
        or the old fattened calf

slaughtered? Cartwheels
    tie one Pan-hoofed season
        to the next, with Bacchus

& Zulus. We believe
    there's pure quartz
        hidden in this room

fretting the light,
    forcing hands to reach
        for each other, beyond

ambrosia. His wife
    seduced by joy & unction,
        wants to know how long

he's danced with a brush
    to will the night's hunger
        into an orgasm of colors.

NUDE STUDY

Someone lightly brushed the penis
    alive. Belief is almost
        flesh. Wings beat,

dust trying to breathe, as if the figure
    might rise from the oils
        & flee the dead

artist's studio. For years
    this piece of work was there
        like a golden struggle

shadowing Thomas McKeller, a black
    elevator operator at the Boston
        Copley Plaza Hotel, a friend

of John Singer Sargent—hidden
    among sketches & drawings, a model
        for Apollo & a bas-relief

of Arion. So much taken
    for granted & denied, only
        grace & mutability

can complete this face belonging
to Greek bodies castrated
with a veil of dust.

AT THE RED SEA

So, this is where
        cries come to us,
                where molting seagulls

peck the air. I never
        thought Crown Heights
                would be so quiet, just

a cantor & a blues singer
        weaving all the old begats
                into Cato, Yankel, Andy,

Michael, James . . . all the others
        transplanted to earthen dams
                & tenements. Sabbath-breakers

& charlatans sow seeds to kill
        fruit. What we forgot
                or never knew is enough

to teach the ant to profane
        sugar. To see injustice,
                don't care where your feet

are planted, you must be
        able to nail your left hand
                to a tree in full bloom.

Now, look at Sheba
        in Solomon's hanging garden,
                carved by grace from head

to toe, she was "wounded
        by love of wisdom" hidden
                in a cloud of galbanum

& myrrh. Didn't the King
        trust his heart? Let's hope
                the crystal floor

over that silent stream
        had nothing to do with
                the color of her skin,

but to prove her legs
        weren't like a donkey's.
                We sense what we've done

even if we can't say why
        we're dismayed or overjoyed
                by how the stones fit

in our hands. The egg
        & sperm we would love
                to deny, they still move

the blood till we can hear,
    "I am black but comely,
        ye daughters of Jerusalem."

Some of us grow ashamed
    peering up from the rat's hole
      in the belly of the Ark

till we're no longer the same
    women & men. Like Sheba
      & Solomon, who asked

hard questions, we know
    if a man is only paid
      a stud fee,

he'll butt his head
    till stars rain down
      & kill some stranger.

As if the night
    on Fire Island
        never happened—the dune

buggy that cut
    like a scythe of moonlight
        across the sand—I see

Frank O'Hara
    with Mapplethorpe's
        book of photographs.

He whistles "Lover
    Man" beneath his breath,
        nudging that fearful

40th year into the background,
    behind those white waves
        of sand. A quick

lunch at Moriarty's
    with someone called LeRoi,
        one of sixty best friends

in the city. He's hurting
    to weigh Melville's concept
        of evil against Henry

James. That woman begging
    a nickel has multiplied
        one hundredfold since

he last walked past the House
    of Seagram. They speak
        of Miles Davis

clubbed twelve times
    outside Birdland by a cop,
        & Frank flips through pages

of Mapplethorpe as if searching
    for something to illustrate
        the cop's real fear.

A dog for the exotic—
    is this what he meant?
        The word Nubian

takes me to monuments
    in Upper Egypt, not
        the "kiss of birds

at the end of the penis"
    singing in the heart
        of America. Julie Harris

merges with images of Bob Love
        till *East of Eden* is
            a compendium of light

& dark. Is this O'Hara's
        Negritude? The phallic temple
            throbs like someone

breathing on calla lilies
        to open them: Leda's
            room of startled mouths.

LINGUA FRANCA

Those double shotgun
          houses in New Orleans
                    can get a man killed.

Helena suns in our shared
          courtyard in her crimson
                    swimsuit. Her breasts

point toward my back
          door, just mesh & light
                    between us. I want to

talk about friendship,
          about how an August day's
                    brightness can murder.

She lies against the ground,
          moving her hips to the music,
                    reading Joaquim Machado

de Assis again. Whispered
          Portuguese floats to me
                    through magnolia scent.

We listen to Afro-Cuban
　　because we both can move
　　　　to the drum. Her husband

is draped in computer cables
　　somewhere. I want to say
　　　　that de Assis's skin color

didn't have anything to do
　　with indelible printing ink
　　　　on his hands, that "Mosca

Azul" & "Circulo Viciosi"
　　had been woven into one
　　　　unbroken song of colors

in my head. The blue
　　fly's "wings of gold
　　　　& Carmine" were also

the glowworm's lament
　　about the sky, the sun's
　　　　wish to be a glowworm.

I want to tell her how
　　she's wounded me with
　　　　red cloth, but before

I can walk across the room
　　a ghost or guardian angel
　　　　slams the door shut.

DESECRATION

The swastika tattooed
on his right bicep & a nude
on his left quiver-dance

as he tries to blowtorch
St. Maurice of Agaunum
off Saxony's coat of

arms. When the flame
spits a molten bead
of blue on his steel-toed

boots, obscenities
leap into the bruised
night. Since his buddy

Awesome chickened out,
he wonders if the picture
in the Alte Pinakothek

would have been easier.
Now that he's started,
where does he stop,

does he go to Coburg,
    Cracow, the Cathedral
        of Lucerne, Schwarzkopf

in Riga, the cloth makers
    & dyers, the tomb of Archbishop
        Ernest at Magdeburg, where

next? He hums a verse
    from Bone Thugs-N-Harmony,
        punching the air as if to break

the saint's armor. Well,
    his ex-girlfriend, Blanche,
        she would know what to do,

how to calm him down
    when he begins to whimper
        & cut initials into his skin.

LOVE IN THE

TIME OF WAR

The jawbone of an ass. A shank
braided with shark teeth. A garrote.
A shepherd's sling. A jagged stone
that catches light & makes warriors
dance to a bull-roarer's lamentation.
An obsidian ax. A lion-skin drum
& reed flute. A nightlong prayer
to gods stopped at the mouth of a cave.

The warrior-king summons one goddess
after another to his bloodstained pallet.
If these dear ones live inside his head
they still dress his wounds with balms
& sacred leaves, & kiss him
back to strength, back to a boy.

Gilgamesh's Humbaba was a distant drum
pulsing among the trees, a slave to the gods,
a foreign tongue guarding the sacred cedars
down to a pale grubworm in the tower
before Babel. Invisible & otherworldly,
he was naked in the king's heart,
& his cry turned flies into maggots
& blood reddened the singing leaves.

When Gilgamesh said Shiduri, a foreplay
of light was on the statues going to the river
between them & the blinding underworld.
She cleansed his wounds & bandaged his eyes
at the edge of reason, & made him forget
birthright, the virgins in their bridal beds.

It seems we all need something to kill
for, to seek & claim, to treasure
till it screams in elemental dark,
to argue with the gods over—
a delicacy or something forbidden—
even if it's only the sooty tern's egg
on Easter Island, as warriors swung ironwood clubs
to topple clans of stony monoliths.

Women danced around a canoe dripping the sap
of the island's last great tree. For the new ruler
who found the season's first egg, whose eyes
reflected obsidian knives & spearheads,
a maiden dressed in a garment of blossoms
waited beneath a towering statue at dusk.

Here, the old masters of Shock & Awe
huddle in the war room, talking iron,
fire & sand, alloy & nomenclature.
Their hearts lag against the bowstring
as they daydream of Odysseus's bed.
But to shoot an arrow through the bull's-eye
of twelve axes lined up in a row
is to sleep with one's eyes open. Yes,

of course, there stands lovely Penelope
like a trophy, still holding the brass key
against her breast. How did the evening star
fall into that room? Lost between plot
& loot, the plucked string turns into a lyre
humming praises & curses to the unborn.

The Mameluke—slave & warrior—springs
out of dust & chance, astride his horse
at sunrise, one with its rage & gallop,
wedded to its flanks & the sound of hooves
striking clay & stone, carried into the sway
of desert grass. His double-edged saber
bloodies valleys & hills, a mirage,
till he arrives at a gate of truth in myth:
for a woman to conceive in this place & time,
she must be in the arms of a warrior riding
down through the bloody ages,
over bones of the enemy in the sand
& along the river in a sultan's dream,
till their child is born on horseback.

Did a Byzantine general intone *Ah!*
when he saw a volcano shoot flames up
across hills? Is nature the master of war?
Could a fissure become a stone syringe
pluming liquid fire against an enemy? Hell
was a beauteous glow made of naphtha,
what the Babylonians called *the thing
that blazes*—oil seeping out of the earth.

If a woman heard the secrets of Greek fire
in a soldier's dream, he couldn't save her.
Only lilies dared to open their pale throats.
After a turtledove spoke on her behalf,
the executioner couldn't believe how light
his hands were, how heavy the ax was.

My wide hips raised two warriors
from sweat & clay, blood sonata
& birth cry. I said anger & avarice,
& they called themselves Cain & Abel.
I said gold, & they opened up the earth.
I said love, & they ventured east
& west, south & north. I said evil,
& they lost themselves in reflected rivers.

After scrimmages across Asia Minor
& guarding kingly ransom in the Horn of Africa,
my sons journeyed home to peasant bread
& salt meat, to whorish doubts & wonder,
but when I flung my arms open at the threshold
they came to me as unseasoned boys.

They swarmed down over the town
& left bodies floating in the ditches
& moats. Bloated with silence,
blue with flies on the rooftops.

They gave the children candy
made of honey & nuts, scented with belladonna
to weed out the weak. Bundles of silk
rolled out like a rainbow for the women.

On the wild forgetful straw beds
they created a race, a new tongue
to sing occidental prayers & regrets.

Their camphor lanterns mastered darkness.
All the taboos of lovemaking were broken.
Soon, laughter rose again from the fields.

Now, she moves against him
like salmon trying to swim upstream
against the earth's spin. The whole night
trembles, the oldest sobs caught

in their throats, a new skin of sweat.
For him, his trek into the deep woods
began days ago when the birds grew silent.
They now pray a son hides inside her.

But tomorrow—tomorrow, only the men
will dance ancestors alive, gazing up at Venus,
born to slay the enemy in their sleep.

The high priest has blessed the weapons,
& they cannot turn back. Not until
a thousand hooves strike the dust red.

The drummer's hands were bloody.
The players of billowy bagpipes
marched straight into the unblinking
muzzle flash. The fife player
conjured a way to disappear
inside himself: The bullets zinged
overhead & raised dust devils
around his feet. He crossed a river.

Bloodstained reeds quivered in the dark.
He rounded a hedgerow thick with blooms
& thorns. Some lone, nameless bird
fell in tune with his fife, somewhere
in the future, & he saw a blue nightgown
fall to the floor of an eye-lit room.

The matador hides the shiny sword
behind his cape & bows to the bull.
Silence kneels in the dung-scented dust.
El toro charges. The matador's quick
two-step is perfecto, as the horns
graze his shadow. He bows again
to the minotaur. Where did the blade
come from, how did it enter the heart?

The flamenco dancer's red skirt catches light
& falls. She adores the levity of his hands
& feet. Some beings steal sunrises
from blood. He knows where the words
come from, that line of García Lorca's
about eating the grasses of the cemeteries?

Hand-to-hand: the two hugged each other
into a naked tussle, one riding the other's back,
locked in a double embrace. One
forced the other to kiss the ground,

as he cursed & bit into an earlobe.
They shook beads of dew off the grass.
One worked his fingers into the black soil,
& could feel a wing easing out of his scapula.

That night, the lucky one who gripped
a stone like Mercury weighing the planet
in his palm, who knew windfall & downfall,

he fell against his sweetheart again
& again, as if holding that warrior in his arms,
& couldn't stop himself from rising off the earth.

Two memories filled the cockpit.
The pilot fingered the samurai swords
beside him, as the plane banked & dove.
Locked in a fire-spitting tailspin,
headed toward the ship, he was one
with the metal & speed, beyond oaths
taken, nose-diving into the huddle
of sailors below, into their thunder.

The day opened like a geisha's pearl fan.
The yellow kimono of his first & last woman
withered into a tangle of cherry blossoms
& breathy silk. A sigh leapt out of his throat.
Before he climbed up into the cockpit
he left a shadow to guard her nights.

Another column of soldiers crosses
the two rivers of flesh & idiom,
time & legacy. An echo of cries
reaches deep into the interior.

Weeks. Months. How many years
of candlepower did it take to journey
from wooden catapult to predator drone
speeding across cerulean sky like sperm?

How many ghosts hide in Liberty's mirror,
how many are released as she strolls
along these deliberate avenues? Oh,

those broken vows & treaties that swear
the only excuse for pig iron & smallpox
is the goodness of gold in the hard earth.

Tribe. Clan. Valley & riverbank. Country. Continent. Interstellar
aborigines. Squad. Platoon. Company. Battalion. Regiment. Hive
& swarm. Colony. Legend. Laws. Ordinances. Statutes. Grid
coordinates. Maps. Longitude. Latitude. Property lines drawn
in unconsecrated dust. Sextant & compass. Ledger. Loyalty
oath. Therefore. Hereinbefore. Esprit de corps. Lock & load.
Bull's-eye. Maggie's drawers. Little Boy. Fat Man. Circle
in the eye. Bayonet. Skull & Bone. Them. Body count. Thou

& I. Us. Honey. Darling. Sweetheart, was I talking war in my sleep
again? Come closer. Yes, place your head against my chest.
The moon on a windowsill. I want to stitch up all your wounds
with kisses, but I also know that sometimes the seed is hurting
for red in the soil. Sometimes. Sometimes I hold you like Achilles'
shield, your mouth on mine, my trembling inside your heart & sex.

When our hands caress bullets & grenades,
or linger on the turrets & luminous wings
of reconnaissance planes, we leave glimpses
of ourselves on the polished hardness.
We surrender skin, hair, sweat, & fingerprints.
The assembly lines hum to our touch,
& the grinding wheels record our laments
& laughter into the bright metal.

I touch your face, your breasts, the flower
holding a world in focus. We give ourselves
to each other, letting the workday slide
away. Afterwards, lying there facing the sky,
I touch the crescent-shaped war wound. Yes,
the oldest prayer is still in my fingertips.

A curtain of fire hangs in the west.
The big gun speaks. Speaks
as if all the gods are cursing at once.
Another timber kneels in the dirt.

I sit at this blue window
entranced by Van Gogh's night sky
burning, as beautiful insanities
skirt the worm-riddled trenches.

The slightest lull beckons GIs
to our doors. Oh, yes, the horses
I've broken in each lonesome body.

I'm the wave ridden beyond chance.
He falls asleep. I whisper into his ear,
& he tells me every signal & secret code.

A marine writes the name of his sweetheart,
carefully printing each letter
as if to make the dead read
the future's blank testaments.

He straddles the fan-tailed bomb
& scribbles a note to al-Qaeda:
This is a fat prick for you sand niggers.
This is a cauldron of falling stars.

Months tick down to a naked sigh.
The marine reads again the Dear John
to bring kisses to life on smudged paper.

Her skin is now a lost map. Each page
is a bloody memory facing itself,
seeping through a white dress.

A bottle-nosed dolphin swims midnight water
with plastic explosives strapped to her body.
A black clock ticks in her half-lit brain.
Brighter than some water-headed boy
in a dream, she calls from the depths. The voice
of her trainer, a Navy SEAL, becomes a radio wave
guiding her to the target. One eye is asleep
& the other is the bright side of the moon.

The trainer & his wife sway to the rise & fall
of their waterbed, locked in each other's arms.
They're taken down into a breathless country
where Neptune wrestles the first & last siren,
to where a shadow from that other world
torpedoes along like a fat, long bullet.

Now you're home, Johnny Boy,
holding me in your arms, I can say
my own peace. How could you lie
to yourself? Democracy & freedom
overseas, my foot. Hanging white fire
& roadside bombs. I still remember
that Saturday you kicked a vet's tin cup
on the corner of Tenth & Avenue A.

Johnny Boy, your kisses may x-through
other names, but I haven't forgotten the night
you were wearing your dress blues & said,
Ladies, line up for this uniform. Your hands
have almost stolen my breath, but I know
a suburban sunset could never heal your red horizon.

Tonight, the old hard work of love
has given up. I can't unbutton promises
or sing secrets into your left ear
tuned to quivering plucked strings.

No, please. I can't face the reflection
of metal on your skin & in your eyes,
can't risk weaving new breath into war fog.
The anger of the trees is rooted in the soil.

Let me drink in your newly found river
of sighs, your way with incantations.
Let me see if I can't string this guitar

& take down your effigy of moonlight
from the cross, the dogwood in bloom
printed on memory's see-through cloth.

A throng of boy soldiers dance
the highlife on a dusty back road
dressed as women, lost in cocaine
happiness, firing Kalashnikovs.

The skinny dogs can smell death
in the twilit alleys. The women
& girls disappear when weaverbirds
desert the tall grandfather trees.

After fetishes are questioned, the guns
run amok. Ghosts patrol the perimeter
& night tries to mend broken rooms.

The women & girls return to the village
with a rebel army hiding inside them.
The gods climb higher into the trees.

I am Abeer Quassim Hamza al-Janabi.
I am one thousand years old.
Once, a long time ago, the Tigris
flowed through me as I gazed up at the sky.
The eyes of the soldiers made me look
at the ground. They followed me in sleep,
hungry dust-birds calling. Now, I am ash,
a bundle of the night's jasmine blossoms

& beliefs. There's a pain inside of me,
but I don't know where. When soldiers
knocked on the door, our house broke
into pieces. There were a thousand dreams
inside me. They tried to burn the evidence,
but I'll always—always be almost fifteen.

Someone's beating a prisoner.
Someone's counting red leaves
falling outside a clouded window
in a secret country. Someone
holds back a river, but the next rabbit jab
makes him piss on the stone floor.
The interrogator orders the man
to dig his grave with a teaspoon.

The one he loves, her name
died last night on his tongue.
To revive it, to take his mind off
the electric wire, he almost said,
There's a parrot in a blue house
that knows the password, a woman's name.

His name is called. A son's lost voice
hovers near a fishing hole in August.
His name is called. A lover's hand
disturbs a breath of summer cloth.
His name is called a third time,
but his propped-up boots & helmet
refuse to answer. The photo remains silent,
& his name hangs in the high rafters.

She tenderly hugs the pillow,
whispering his name. The dog
rises beside the bedroom door
& wanders to the front door,
& stands with its head cocked,
listening for a name in a dead language.

WARHORSES

THE HELMET

Perhaps someone was watching
a mud turtle or an armadillo
skulk along an old interminable footpath,
armored against sworn enemies,
& then that someone shaped a model,
nothing but the mock-up of a hunch
into a halved, rounded, carved-out
globe of wood covered with animal skin.
How many battles were fought before
bronze meant shield & breastplate,
before iron was fired, hammered, & taught
to outwit the brain's glacial weather,
to hold an edge? God-inspired,
it was made to deflect a blow
or blade, to make the light pivot
on the battlefield. Did the soldiers
first question this new piece of equipment,
did they laugh like a squad of Hells Angels,
saying, Is this our ration bowl for bonemeal,
& gore? The commander's sunrise
was stolen from the Old Masters,
& his coat of arms made the shadows
kneel. The ram, the lion, the ox,
the goat—folkloric. Horse-headed
helmets skirted the towering cedars
till only a lone vulture circled the sky
as first & last decipher of the world.

GRENADE

There's no rehearsal to turn flesh into dust so quickly. A hair trigger, a cocked hammer in the brain, a split second between a man & infamy. It lands on the ground—a few soldiers duck & the others are caught in a half run—& one throws himself down on the grenade. All the watches stop. A flash. Smoke. Silence. The sound fills the whole day. Flesh & earth fall into the eyes & mouths of the men. A dream trapped in mid-air. They touch their legs & arms, their groins, ears, & noses, saying, What happened? Some are crying. Others are laughing. Some are almost dancing. Someone tries to put the dead man back together. "He just dove on the damn thing, sir!" A flash. Smoke. Silence. The day blown apart. For those who can walk away, what is their burden? Shreds of flesh & bloody rags gathered up & stuffed into a bag. Each breath belongs to him. Each song. Each curse. Every prayer is his. Your body doesn't belong to your mind & soul. Who are you? Do you remember the man left in the jungle? The others who owe their lives to this phantom, do they feel like you? Would his loved ones remember him if that little park or statue erected in his name didn't exist, & does it enlarge their lives? You wish he'd lie down in that closed coffin, & not wander the streets or enter your bedroom at midnight. The woman you love, she'll never understand. Who would? You remember what he used to say: "If you give a kite too much string, it'll break free." That unselfish certainty. But you can't remember when you began to live his unspoken dreams.

THE TOWERS

Yes, dear son
dead, but not gone,
some were good, ordinary
people who loved a pinch of salt
on a slice of melon. Good,
everyday souls gazing up
at birds every now & then,
a flash of wings like blood
against the skylights. Well,
others were good as gold
certificates in a strongbox
buried in the good earth. Yes,
two or three stopped to give
the homeless vet on the corner
a shiny quarter or silver dime,
while others walked dead
into a fiery brisance, lost
in an eternity of Vermeer.
A few left questions blighting
the air. Does she love me?
How can I forgive him?
Why does the dog growl
when I turn the doorknob?
Some were writing e-mails
& embossed letters to ghosts
when the first plane struck.
The boom of one thousand
trap drums was thrown against
a metallic sky. A century of blue
vaults opened, & rescue workers
scrambled with their lifelines
down into the dark, sending up
plumes of disbelieving dust.
They tried to soothe torn earth,
to stretch skin back over the
pulse beat. When old doubts
& shame burn, do they smell
like anything we've known?
When happiness is caught off
guard, when it beats its wings
bloody against the bony cage,
does it die screaming or laughing?

No,
none,
not a single one
possessed wings as agile
& unabashedly decorous as yours,
son. Not even those lovers who
grabbed each other's hand & leapt
through the exploding windows.
Pieces of sky fell with the glass,
bricks, & charred mortar. Nothing
held together anymore. Machines
grunted & groaned into the heap
like gigantic dung beetles. After
planes had flown out of a scenario
in Hollywood, few now believed
their own feet touched the ground.
Signed deeds & promissory notes
floated over the tangled streets,
& some hobbled in broken shoes
toward the Brooklyn Bridge.
The cash registers stopped on
decimal points, in a cloud bank
of dead cell phones & dross.
Search dogs crawled into tombs
of burning silence. September
could hardly hold itself upright,
but no one donned any feathers.
Apollo was at Ground Zero
because he knows everything
about bandaging up wounds.
Men dug hands into quavering
flotsam, & they were blinded by
the moon's indifference. No,
Voice, I don't know anything
about infidels, though I can see
those men shaving their bodies
before facing a malicious god
in the mirror. The searchlights
throbbed. No, I'm not Daedalus,
but I've walked miles in a circle,
questioning your wings of beeswax
& crepe singed beyond belief.

HEAVY METAL SOLILOQUY

After a nightlong white-hot hellfire
of blue steel, we rolled into Baghdad,
plugged into government-issued earphones,
hearing hard rock. The drum machines
& revved-up guitars roared in our heads.
All their gods were crawling on all fours.
These bloated replicas of horned beetles
drew us to targets, as if they could breathe
& think. The turrets rotated 360 degrees.
The infrared scopes could see through stone.
There were mounds of silver in the oily dark.
Our helmets were the only shape of the world.
Lightning was inside our titanium tanks,
& the music was almost holy, even if blood
was now leaking from our eardrums.
We were moving to a predestined score
as bodies slumped under the bright heft
& weight of thunderous falling sky.
Locked in, shielded off from desert sand
& equatorial eyes, I was inside a womb,
a carmine world, caught in a limbo,
my finger on the trigger, getting ready to die,
getting ready to be born.

He has bribed the thorns
to guard his poppies.
They intoxicate the valley
with their forbidden scent,
reddening the horizon
till it is almost as if
they aren't there.
Maybe the guns guard
only the notorious
dreams in his head.
The weather is kind
to every bloom,
& the fat greenish bulbs
form a galaxy of fantasies
& beautiful nightmares.
After they're harvested
& molded into kilo sacks
of malleable brown powder,
they cross the country
on horseback,
on river rafts
following some falling star,
& then ride men's shoulders
down to the underworld,
down to rigged scales

where money changers
& gunrunners linger
in the pistol-whipped hush
of broad daylight. No,
now, it shouldn't be long
before the needle's bright tip
holds a drop of woeful bliss,
before the fifth horseman of the Apocalypse
gallops again the night streets of Europe.

SURGE

Always more. No, we aren't too ashamed to prod celestial beings
into our machines. Always more body bags & body counts for oath takers
& sharpshooters. Always more. More meat for the gibbous grinder
& midnight mover. There's always someone standing on a hill, half lost
behind dark aviation glasses, saying, If you asked me, buddy, you know,
it could always be worse. A lost arm & leg? Well, you could be stone dead.
Here comes another column of apparitions to dig a lifetime of roadside
    graves.
Listen to the wind beg. Always more young, strong, healthy bodies.
    Always.

Yes. What a beautiful golden sunset. (*A pause*) There's always that one
    naked soul
who'll stand up, shuffle his feet a little, & then look the auspicious,
    would-be gods
in the eyes & say, Enough! I won't give another good guess or black
    thumbnail
to this mad dream of yours! An ordinary man or woman. Alone. A
    mechanic
or cowboy. A baker. A farmer. A hard hat. A tool-&-die man. Almost a
    smile
at the corners of a mouth. A fisherman. A tree surgeon. A seamstress.
    Someone.

Although the sandy soil's already red,
the devil still comes on horseback
at midnight, with old obscenities
in his head, galloping along a pipeline
that ferries oil to the black tankers
headed for Shanghai. Traveling
through folklore & songs, prayers
& curses, he's a windmill of torches
& hot lead, rage & plunder, bloodlust
& self-hatred, rising out of the Seven Odes,
a Crow of the Arabs. Let them wing
& soar, let them stumble away on broken feet,
let them beg with words of the unborn,
let them strum a dusty oud of gut & gourd,
still the devil rides a shadow at daybreak.
Pity one who doesn't know his bloodline
is rape. He rides with a child's heart
in his hands, a head on a crooked staff,
& he can't stop charging the night sky
till his own dark face turns into ashes
riding a desert wind's mirage.

FROM "AUTOBIOGRAPHY OF MY ALTER EGO"

You see these eyes?
                              You see this tongue?
You see these ears?
                              They may detect a quiver
in the grass, an octave
                              higher or lower—
a little different, an iota,
                              but they're no different
than your eyes & ears.
                              I can't say I don't know
how Lady Liberty's
                              tilted in my favor or yours,
that I don't hear what I hear
                              & don't see what I see
in the cocksure night
                              from Jefferson & Washington
to terrorists in hoods & sheets
                              in a black man's head.
As he feels what's happening
                              you can also see & hear
what's happening to him.
                              You see these hands?
They know enough to save us.
                              I'm trying to say this: True,

I'm a cover artist's son,
                              born to read between lines,
but I also know that you know
                              a whispered shadow in the trees
is the collective mind
                              of insects, birds, & animals
witnessing what we do to each other.

                              *

Forgive the brightly colored
                              viper on the footpath,
guarding a forgotten shrine.
                              Forgive the tiger
dumbstruck beneath its own rainbow.
                              Forgive the spotted bitch
eating her litter underneath the house.
                              Forgive the boar
hiding in October's red leaves.
                              Forgive the stormy century
of crows calling to death. Forgive
                              the one who conjures a god
out of spit & clay
                              so she may seek redemption.
Forgive the elephant's memory.
                              Forgive the saw vine
& the thorn bird's litany.
                              Forgive the schizoid
gatekeeper, his logbook's
                              perfect excuse. Forgive

the crocodile's swiftness.
                                Forgive the pheromones
& the idea of life on Mars.
                                Forgive the heat lightning
& the powder keg. Forgive the raccoon's
                                        sleight of hand beside
the river. Forgive the mooncalf
                                & doubt's caul-baby. Forgive
my father's larcenous tongue.
                                Forgive my mother's intoxicated
lullaby. Forgive my sixth sense.
                                Forgive my heart & penis,
but don't forgive my hands.

THE

CHAMELEON

COUCH

CANTICLE

Because I mistrust my head & hands, because I know salt
    tinctures my songs, I tried hard not to touch you
even as I pulled you into my arms. Seasons sprouted
    & went to seed as we circled the dance with silver cat bells
tied to our feet. Now, kissing you, I am the arch-heir of second chances.
    Because I know twelve ways to be wrong
& two to be good, I was wounded by the final question in the cave,
    left side of the spirit level's quiver. I didn't want to hug you
into a cross, but I'm here to be measured down to each numbered bone.
    A trembling runs through what pulls us to the blood knot.
We hold hands & laugh in the East Village as midnight autumn
    shakes the smoke of the Chicago B.L.U.E.S. club from our clothes,
& you say I make you happy & sad. For years I stopped my hands
    in midair, knowing fire at the root stem of yes.
I say your name, & another dies in my mouth because I know how to plead
    till a breeze erases the devil's footprints,
because I crave something to sing the blues about. Look,
    I only want to hold you this way: a bundle of wild orchids
broken at the wet seam of memory & manna.

The day breaks in half as the sun rolls over hanging ice,
& a dogwood leans into a country between seasons.
A yellow cat looms with feet in the squishy snow,
arching her back, eyeing a redbird, a star still blinking
in her nighttime brain. Schoolgirls sport light dresses
beneath heavy coats, & the boys stand goose-pimpled
in football jerseys. Anything for a hug or kiss,
anything to be healed. A new-green leaf swells sap.
Each bud is a nose pressed against a windowpane,
a breast gazing through thin cotton. The cold stings,
& a shiver goes from crown to feet, leaf tip down to taproot.
The next-door boy's snowman bows to Monday's rush hour.
Heavy metal leaps from a car & ignites the spluttering air.
Each little tight fist of clutched brightness begins to open,
distant & close as ghost laughter in the afternoon.
A crow sits on the fence, telling me how many ways
to answer its brutal questions about tomorrow.
The season is a white buffalo birthing in the front yard:
big-eyed with beauty, half out & half in.
Branches cluster with mouths ready to speak
a second coming, & a wind off the Delaware
springs forth, rattling the window sashes.
An all-night howl slips beneath the eaves,
& next day, frozen buds are death's-heads
fallen into footprints coming & gone.

IGNIS FATUUS

Something or someone. A feeling
among a swish of reeds. A swampy
glow haloes the Spanish moss,
& there's a swaying at the edge
like a child's memory of abuse
growing flesh, living on what
a screech owl recalls. Nothing
but a presence that fills up
the mind, a replenished body
singing its way into double-talk.
In the city, "Will o' the Wisp"
floats out of Miles's trumpet,
leaning ghosts against nighttime's
backdrop of neon. A foolish fire
can also start this way: before
you slide the key into the lock
& half turn the knob, you know
someone has snuck into your life.
A high window, a corner of sky
spies on upturned drawers of underwear
& unanswered letters, on a tin box
of luminous buttons & subway tokens,
on books, magazines, & clothes
flung to the studio's floor,
his sweat still owning the air.

Years ago you followed someone
here, in love with breath
kissing the nape of your neck,
back when it was easy to be
at least two places at once.

A TRANSLATION OF SILK

One can shove his face against silk
& breathe in centuries of perfume
on the edge of a war-torn morning
where men fell so hard for iron
they could taste it. Now, today,
a breeze disturbs a leafy pagoda
printed on slow cloth. A creek
begins to move. His brain trails,
lagging behind his fingers to learn
suggestion is more than radiance
shaped to the memory of hands,
that one of the smallest creatures
knows how to be an impressive god.
A flounce of light is the only praise
it ever receives. I need to trust
this old way of teaching a man
to cry, & I want to believe in
what's left of the mulberry leaves.
Humans crave immortality, but oh,
yes, to think worms wove this
as a way to stay alive in our world.

DEAD RECKONING

Fishermen follow a dream of the biggest
catch, out among the tall waves where
freshwater meets a salty calmness.
For hundreds of years they've crossed
this body of water, casting their nets
& singing old songs. They've slept
with the village women & ridden waves
back to the other side to loved ones.
Now, lost in the old clothes of unreason
& wanderlust, their nets sag with the last
of its kind, with bountiful fish stories,
& soon the flirtatious mermaids are
beckoning from a swoon of reeds,
calling their names. The first dance
is desire. The second dance is love.
The tall grass quivers like a siren
snagged in a shabby net. Now,
as if on a journey of lost souls,
love & desire dance with death,
twirling bright skirts till flesh & cloth
turn into ashes. What did they do
to make the gods angry? Forbidden
laughter of the mermaids fills the night,
& if humans try to sing this laughter,
their voices only cry out in the dark.

CAPE COAST CASTLE

I made love to you, & it loomed there.
We sat on the small veranda of the cottage,
& listened hours to the sea talk.
I didn't have to look up to see if it was still there.
For days, it followed us along polluted beaches
where the boys herded cows
& the girls danced for the boys,
to the money changer,
& then to the marketplace.
It went away when the ghost of my mother
found me sitting beneath a palm,
but was in the van with us on a road trip to the country
as we zoomed past thatch houses.
It was definitely there when a few dollars
exchanged hands & we were hurried
through customs, past the guards.
I was standing in the airport in Amsterdam,
sipping a glass of red wine, half lost in Van Gogh's
swarm of colors, & it was there, brooding in a corner.
I walked into the public toilet, thinking of W. E. B.
buried in a mausoleum, & all his books & papers
going to dust, & there it was, in that private moment,
the same image: obscene because it was built
to endure time, stronger than their houses & altars.
The seeds of melon. The seeds of gumbo in trade winds

headed to a new world. I walked back into the throng
of strangers, but it followed me. I could see the path
slaves traveled, & I knew when they first saw it
all their high gods knelt on the ground.
Why did I taste salt water in my mouth?
We stood in line for another plane,
& when the plane rose over the city
I knew it was there, crossing the Atlantic.
Not a feeling, but a longing. I was in Accra
again, gazing up at the vaulted cathedral ceiling
of the compound. I could see the ships at dusk
rising out of the lull of "Amazing Grace," cresting
the waves. The governor stood on his balcony,
holding a sword, pointing to a woman
in the courtyard, saying, That one.
Bring me that tall, ample wench.
Enslaved hands dragged her to the center,
then they threw buckets of water on her,
but she tried to fight. They pinned her to the ground.
She was crying. They prodded her up the stairs. One step,
& then another. Oh, yeah, she still had some fight in her,
but the governor's power was absolute. He said,
There's a tyranny of language in my fluted bones.
There's poetry on every page of the Good Book.
There's God's work to be done in a forsaken land.
There's a whole tribe in this one, but I'll break them
before they're in the womb, before they're conceived,
before they're even thought of. Come, up here,
don't be afraid, up here to the governor's quarters,
up here where laws are made. I haven't delivered

the head of Pompey or John the Baptist
on a big silver tray, but I own your past,
present, & future. You're special.
You're not like the others. Yes,
I'll break you with fists & cat-o'-nine.
I'll thoroughly break you, head to feet,
but, sister, I'll break you most dearly
with sweet words.

BLACK FIGS

Because they tasted so damn good, I swore
    I'd never eat another one, but three seedy little hearts
beckoned tonight from a green leaf-shaped saucer,
    swollen with ripeness, ready to spill a gutty
sacrament on my tongue. Their skins too smooth
    to trust or believe. Shall I play Nat King Cole's
"Nature Boy" or Cassandra's "Death Letter"
    this Gypsy hour? I have a few words to steal
back the taste of earth. I know laughter can rip
    stitches, & deeds come undone in the middle of a dance.
Socrates talked himself into raising the cup to his lips
    to toast the avenging oracle, but I told the gods no
false kisses, they could keep their ambrosia & nectar,
    & let me live my days & nights. I nibble each globe,
each succulent bud down to its broken-off stem
    like a boy trying to make a candy bar last
the whole day, & laughter unlocks my throat
    when a light falls across Bleecker Street
against the ugly fire escape.

FATA MORGANA

I could see thatch boats. The sea
swayed against falling sky. Mongolian
horses crested hills, helmets edging the perimeter,
& I saw etched on the horizon scarab insignias.
The clangor of swords & armor echoed
& frightened scorpions into their holes,
& the question of zero clouded the brain.
I saw three faces of my death foretold.
I sat at a table overflowing with muscadine & quince,
but never knew a jealous husband poisoned the Shiraz.
I laughed at his old silly joke about Caligula
lounging in a bathhouse made of salt blocks.
I was on a lost ship near the equator,
& only a handful of us were still alive,
cannibal judgment in our eyes.
I came to a restful valley of goats & dragon lizards,
but only thought of sand spilling from my boots.
I witnessed the burning of heretics near an oasis,
& dreamt of gulls interrogating sea horses, cuttlefish,
& crabs crawling out of the white dunes.
I could see the queen of scapegoats
donning a mask as palms skirted the valley.
I was lost in a very old land, before Christ
& Muhammad, & when I opened my eyes
I could see women embracing a tribunal

of gasoline cans. I heard a scuttling
on the seafloor. I knew beforehand
what surrender would look like after
long victory parades & proclamations,
& could hear the sounds lovemaking
brought to the cave & headquarters.

ENGLISH

When I was a boy, he says, the sky began burning,
& someone ran knocking on our door
one night. The house became birds
in the eaves too low for a boy's ears.

I heard a girl talking, but they weren't words.
I knew one good thing: a girl
was somewhere in our house,
speaking slow as a sailor's parrot.

I glimpsed Alice in Wonderland.
Her voice smelled like an orange,
though I'd never peeled an orange.
I knocked on the walls, in a circle.

The voice was almost America.
My ears plucked a word out of the air.
She said, Friend. I eased open the door
hidden behind overcoats in a closet.

The young woman was smiling at me.
She was teaching herself a language
to take her far, far away,
& she taught me a word each day to keep secret.

But one night I woke to other voices in the house.
A commotion downstairs & a pleading.
There are promises made at night
that turn into stones at daybreak.

From my window, I saw the stars
burning in the river brighter than a big
celebration. I waited for her return,
with my hands over my mouth.

I can't say her name, because it was
dangerous in our house so close to the water.
Was she a boy's make-believe friend
or a beehive breathing inside the walls?

Years later my aunts said two German soldiers
shot the girl one night beside the Vistula.
This is how I learned your language.
It was long ago. It was springtime.

POPPIES

These frantic blooms can hold their own
when it comes to metaphor & God.
Take any name or shade of irony, any flowery
indifference or stolen gratitude, & our eyes,
good or bad, still run up to this hue.
Take this woman sitting beside me,

a descendant of Hungarian Gypsies
born to teach horses to dance & eat sugar
from her hand, does she know beauty
couldn't have protected her, that a poppy
tucked in her hair couldn't have saved her
from those German storm troopers?

This frightens me. I see eyes peeping
through narrow slats of cattle cars
hurrying toward forever. I see "Jude"
& "Star of David" scribbled across a depot,
but she says, That's the name of a soccer team,
baby. Red climbs the hills & descends,

hurrying out to the edge of a perfect view,
& then another, between white & violet.
It is a skirt or cape flung to the ground.
It is old denial worked into the soil.
It is a hungry new vanity that rises
& then runs up to our bleating train.

I am a black man, a poet, a bohemian,
& there isn't a road my mind doesn't travel.
I also have my cheap, one-way ticket
to Auschwitz & know of no street or footpath
death hasn't taken. The poppies rush ahead,
up to a cardinal singing on barbed wire.

ORPHEUS AT THE
SECOND GATE OF HADES

My lyre has fallen & broken,
but I have my little tom-toms.
Look, do you see those crows
perched on the guardhouse?
I don't wish to speak of omens,
but sometimes it's hard to guess.
Life has been good the past few years.
I know all seven songs of the sparrow,
& I feel lucky to be alive. I woke up at 2:59
this morning reprieved because I fought
dream catchers & won. I'll place a stone
into my mouth & go down there again,
& if I meet myself mounting the stairs
it won't be the same man descending.
Doubt has walked me to the river's edge
before. I may be ashamed, but I can't forget
how to mourn & praise on the marimba.
I shall play till the day's golden machinery
stops between the known & unknown.
The place was a funeral pyre for the young
who died before knowing the thirst of man
or woman. Furies with snakes in their hair
wept. Tantalus ate pears & sipped wine
in a dream, as the eyes of a vulture

poised over Tityus's liver. I could see
Ixion strapped to a gyrating wheel
& Sisyphus sat on his rounded stone.
I shall stand again before Proserpine
& King Pluto. When it comes to defending love,
I can make a lyre drag down the moon & stars
but it's still hard to talk of earthly things—
ordinary men killing ordinary men,
women, & children. I don't remember
exactly what I said at the ticket office
my first visit here, but I do know it grew
ugly. The classical allusions didn't
make it any easier. I played a tune
that worked its way into my muscles,
& I knew I had to speak of what I'd seen
before the serpent drew back its head.
I saw a stall filled with human things, an endless
list of names, a hill of shoes, a room of suitcases
tagged to nowhere, eyeglasses, toothbrushes,
baby shoes, dentures, ads for holiday spas,
& a wide roll of thick cloth woven of living hair.
If I never possessed these reed flutes
& drums, if my shadow stops kissing me
because of what I have witnessed,
I shall holler to you through my bones,
I promise you.

THREE FIGURES AT THE
BASE OF A CRUCIFIXION

Look how each pound of meat
manages to climb up & weigh itself
in the wobbly cage of the head.
Did the painter ascend a dogwood
or crawl into the hold of a slave ship
to get a good view of the thing
turning itself inside out beneath
a century of interrogation lamps?

It was always here, hiding behind
gauze, myth, doubt, blood, & spit.
After the exhibit on New Bond Street
they walked blocks around a garden
of April roses, tiger lilies, duckweed,
& trillium, shaking their heads.
The burning of mad silence left
powder rooms & tea parlors smoky.

Brushstrokes formed a blade to cut
the hues. A slipped disk
grew into a counterweight,
& the muse kept saying,

Learn to be kind to yourself.
A twisted globe of flesh
is held together by what
it pushes against.

A VISIT TO INNER SANCTUM

A poet stands on the steps of the grand cathedral,
wondering if he has been a coward in hard times.
He traveled east, north, south, & seven directions
of the west. When he first arrived on the other side
of the sea, before he fell into the flung-open arms
of a long romance, the lemon trees were in bloom.

After a year, poised on the rift of a purple haze,
he forgot all the questions he brought with him.
Couldn't he see the tear gas drifting over Ohio
as flower children danced to Jefferson Airplane?
Will he ever write a sonnet dedicated to the memory
of four girls dynamited in a Birmingham church?

Standing in the cathedral again, in the midst
of what first calibrated his tongue—gold icons
& hidden jaguars etched into the high beams—
he remembers an emanation almost forgotten.
He can't stop counting dead heroes who lived in his head,
sultry refrains that kept him alive in the country of clouds.

Underneath the granite floor where he stands
loom the stone buttresses of an ancient temple.
When he was a boy, with his head bowed
close to the scarred floor, he could hear voices
rising from below, their old lingua franca
binding with his. How could he forget?

Outside the Institute of National Memory
he toasts the gods hiding between stanzas.
The girl he left behind for enemy soldiers
to rough up & frighten, she never stopped
waiting for him, even after she lost herself
in booze. Now he faces a rusty iron gate.

Did she know someday he'd question a life
till he held only a bone at the dull-green door
of an icehouse where they stole their first kiss?
To have laughed beside another sweetheart
in a distant land is to have betrayed the soil
of dispossession hidden under his fingernails.

Suppose he'd pursued other, smaller passions
singing of night dew? The dead ones kept him
almost honest, tangoing with wives of despots
entranced by stolen light in his eyes & hair.
He never wanted to believe a pinch of salt
for a pinch of sugar is how scales are balanced.

UNLIKELY CLAIMS

This is my house. My sweat is in the mortar
& hewn wood. This garden of garlic blooms
is mine too, said last night's pale ghost.
I know every crack where cold & light
try to sneak in, & where the past tongues
& grooves the future. I own every rusty nail.
This fence wasn't here when hobnailed boots
marched us into the night. I remember all
the cat's-eye marbles would roll to this corner
of the kitchen. This tree limb my uncle cut
to make a witching rod. Here's the mark
an anniversary candle left on the counter,
said the ghost, slowly fingering
the deep burn like an old wound.
Now dirt-bike trails crisscross
the apple grove my father planted.
The goat tied beside the back gate
belongs to my progeny of beautiful
goats. You sold the mineral rights
under our feet, but the bird we hear
singing overhead in a Yiddish accent
owns the morning. These roses are mine
because I've walked through fire.
Go & tell your drinking buddies
& psychoanalyst your neighbor

has risen from the ashes. I wonder
if I should tell you about the love letters
hidden behind the doorjamb. This house
still stands among my lavender flowers.
Tell your inheritors to think of me
when they smile up at the sky.

WHEN EYES ARE ON ME

I am a scrappy old lion
who's wandered into a Christian square
quavering with centuries of forged bells.
The cobblestones make my feet ache.

I walk big-shouldered, my head raised
proudly. I smell the blood of a king.
The citizens can see only a minotaur in a maze.
I know more than a lion should know.

My roar goes back to the Serengeti,
to when a savanna was craggy ice,
but now it frightens only pigeons from a city stoop.
They believe they know my brain's contours & grammar.

Don't ask me how I know the signs engraved
on a sundial, the secret icons behind a gaze.
I wish their crimes hadn't followed me here.
I can hear their applause in the dusty citadel.

I know what it took to master the serpent
& wheel, the crossbow & spinal tap.
Once I was a leopard beside a stone gate.
I am a riddle to be unraveled. I am not

& I am. When their eyes are on me
I become whatever is judged badly.
I circle the park. Hunger shapes
my keen sense of smell, a lifetime ahead.

They will follow my pawprints
till they're lost in snow at dusk.
If I walk in circles, I hide from my shadow.
They plot stars to know where to find me.

I am a prodigal bird perched on the peak
of a guardhouse. I have a message
for fate. The sunlight has shown me
the guns, & their beautiful sons are deadly.

BEGOTTEN

I'm the son of poor Mildred & illiterate J.W.
But I sit here with Ninsun's song in my mouth,
knowing the fantastic blue Bull of Heaven
because I've cried at a woman's midnight door
clouded by sea mist. Grief followed me, saying,
Burn your keepsakes, or give them to Goodwill
or the Salvation Army, & then live on the streets.
But I couldn't forget a half-dead, ugly prickly pear
breaking into twenty-three yellow blooms.
Namtar's bird of prey perched on my shoulder
as I wandered darkness searching for light,
knowing, finally, I was born to be hooked
quickly as a fish. To spend an hour in Uruk
tonight is to awake in the Green Zone
with another dictator's lassoed statue
pulled to the ground. The gods count
the dead, running eyes over folly, guilt,
& restitution, saying, Now, dear one,
you are bread. They tally grain & stock
noted in cuneiform, & I hear a whisper:
Bread for Neti, the keeper of the gate,
bread for Ningizzida, the serpent god
& fat lord of the ever-living tree,
& bread for Enmul, bread for all of them.
We dream of going from one desire

to the next. But in the final analysis,
a good thought is the simplest food.
Ninhursag is the mother of creation,
& the ants her most trustful servants
because they are always on their way.

BLUE DEMENTIA

In the days when a man
would hold a swarm of words
inside his belly, nestled
against his spleen, singing.

In the days of night riders
when life tongued a reed
till blues & sorrow song
called out of the deep night:
Another man done gone.
Another man done gone.

In the days when one could lose oneself
all up inside love that way,
& then moan on the bone
till the gods cried out in someone's sleep.

Today,
already I've seen three dark-skinned men
discussing the weather with demons
& angels, gazing up at the clouds
& squinting down into iron grates
along the fast streets of luminous encounters.
I double-check my reflection in plate glass
& wonder, Am I passing another

Lucky Thompson or Marion Brown
cornered by a blue dementia,
another dark-skinned man
who woke up dreaming one morning
& then walked out of himself
dreaming? Did this one dare
to step on a crack in the sidewalk,
to turn a midnight corner & never come back
whole, or did he try to stare down a look
that shoved a blade into his heart?
I mean, I also know something
about night riders & catgut. Yeah,
honey, I know something about talking with ghosts.

GRUNGE

No, sweetheart, I said *courtly love.*
I was thinking of John Donne's
"Yet this enjoys before it woo,"
but my big hands were dreaming
Pinetop's boogie-woogie piano
taking the ubiquitous night apart.
Not Courtney. I know "Inflated Tear"
means worlds approaching pain
& colliding, or a heavenly body
calling to darkness, & that shame
has never been my truest garment,
because I was born afraid of needles.
But I've been shoved up against
frayed ropes too, & I had to learn
to bob & weave, to duck & hook,
till I could jab my way out of
a foregone conclusion, till blues
reddened a room. All I know is,
sometimes a man wants only a hug
when something two-steps him
toward a little makeshift stage.
Somehow, between hellhounds
& a guitar solo made of gutstring
& wood, I outlived a stormy night
with snow on my eyelids.

GREEN

I've known billy club, tear gas, & cattle prod,
but not Black Sheep killing White Sheep.
Or vice versa. I've known water hoses
& the subterranean cry of a Black Maria
rounding a city corner on two angry wheels,
but couldn't smell cedar taking root in the air.

I've known of secret graves guarded
by the night owl in oak & poplar.
I've known police dogs on choke chains.
I've known how "We Shall Overcome"
feels on a half-broken tongue,
but not how deeply sunsets wounded the Peacock Throne.

Because of what I never dreamt
I know Hafez's litany balanced on Tamerlane's saber,
a gholam's song limping up the Elburz Mountains—
no, let's come back first to *now*,
to a surge of voices shouting,
Death to the government of potato!

Back to the iron horses of the Basijis
galloping through days whipped bloody
& beaten back into the brain's cave
louder than a swarm of percussion
clobbered in Enghelab Square,
cries bullied into alleyways & cutoffs.

Though each struck bell goes on
mumbling in the executioner's sleep,
there are always two hands holding
on to earth, & I believe their faith
in tomorrow's million green flags waving
could hold back a mile of tanks & turn

the Revolutionary Guard into stone,
that wherever a clue dares to step
a seed is pressed into damp soil.
A shoot, a tendril, the tip of a wing.
One breath at a time, it holds till it is
uprooted, or torn from its own grip.

THE HEDONIST

I pull on my crow mask.
Butterflies & insects rise
in the ether of remembrance.
I suck all the sappy nectar
from honeysuckle blossoms
fallen in last night's scuffle
between gods & human shadows.

I'd die for October's last juicy plums
beside the shady marsh at the brink.
I'd stand on an anthill to learn
the blue heron's treatise on agony.
Every joy & sorrow are mine.
I bow to kiss a whipping post
so I can taste salt & contrition.

I know all the monsters lurking
in Lord Byron's verses. I follow
beauties up & down Broadway
till their masks own me.
I walk through the city,
saying, What did Kierkegaard know
about love & the God-worm?

After eating quail eggs & fish tongues,
I don a snarling dog mask
& pursue a would-be lover
into the hanging garden
till the Lethe is on her left
& the Styx is on her right,
& then I enter the labyrinth.

My alter ego is my servant.
Bring me fat gooseberries.
Translucent snails in sea salt.
Bring me a bit of Philopator's heart.
I have a taste for the fugu fish
because there's nothing
delicious as chance.

I've stood at a window
overlooking the Ideal City,
mouthing odes to a burnt silver spoon,
to a candle's flame-glut,
to a woman in the distance,
to the insipid angel
on the tip of a needle.

My caul has bitten into me.
I know the eternal earthworm.
Behind my peacock mask,
facing the Adriatic Sea,
I wonder what it would feel like
to follow pearl divers down, to know
the holy pressure of falling water.

HOW IT IS

My muse is holding me prisoner.
She refuses to give back my shadow,
anything that clings to a stone or tree
to keep me here. I recite dead poets
to her, & their words heal the cold air.
I feed her fat, sweet, juicy grapes,
& melons holding a tropical sun
inside them. From here, I see only
the river. The blue heron dives,
& always rises with a bright fish
in its beak, dangling a grace note.
She leans over & whispers, Someday,
I'll find some way to make you cry.
What are her three beautiful faces
telling me? I peel her an orange.
Each slice bleeds open a sigh.
Honeydew perfumes an evening
of black lace & torch songs,
& I bow down inside myself
& walk on my hands & knees
to break our embrace, but can't
escape. I think she knows
I could free myself of the thin gold chain
invisible around her waist,
but if she left the door open,

I'd still be standing here
in her ravenous light.
Her touch is alchemical.
When she questions my love,
I serve her robin's eggs
on a blue plate. She looks me in the eye
& says, You still can't go. Somehow,
I'd forgotten I'm her prisoner,
but I glance over at the big rock
wedged against the back door.
I think she knows, with her kisses
in my mouth, I could walk on water.

I can't erase her voice. If I opened the door to the cage & tossed the magpie into the air, a part of me would fly away, leaving only the memory of a plucked string trembling in the night. The voice unwinds breath, soldered wires, chance, loss, & digitalized impulse. She's telling me how light pushed darkness till her father stood at the bedroom door dressed in a white tunic. Sometimes we all wish we could put words back into our mouths.

I have a plant of hers that has died many times, only to be revived with less water & more light, always reminding me of the voice caught inside the little black machine. She lives between the Vale of Kashmir & nirvana, beneath a bipolar sky. The voice speaks of an atlas & a mask, a map of Punjab, an ugly scar from college days on her abdomen, the unsaid credo, but I still can't make the voice say, Look, I'm sorry. I've been dead for a long time.

TOGETHERNESS

Someone says Tristan
& Isolde, the shared cup
& broken vows binding them,
& someone else says Romeo
& Juliet, a lyre & Jew's harp
sighing a forbidden oath,
but I say a midnight horn
& a voice with a moody angel
inside, the two married rib
to rib. Of course, I am
thinking of those Tuesdays
or Thursdays at Billy Berg's
in L.A. when Lana Turner would say,
Please sing "Strange Fruit"
for me, & then her dancing
nightlong with Mel Tormé,
as if she knew what it took
to make brass & flesh say yes
beneath the clandestine stars
& a spinning that is so fast
we can't feel the planet moving.
Is this why some of us fall
in & out of love? Did Lady Day
& Prez ever hold each other
& plead to those notorious gods?

I don't know. But I do know
even if a horn & voice plumb
the unknown, what remains unsaid
coalesces around an old blues
& begs with a hawk's yellow eyes.

DEAR MISTER DECOY

If it weren't for you, I wouldn't be
    smooth as morning light on cold stone.
I walk into a jewelry store ten paces behind you
    & look them in the eye like a pawnbroker
when I wear this apple-red lipstick
    & blush of Icelandic rouge.
I lean lightly on the showcase in a low-cut
    flair of tailored innocence. You could be
the lost descendant of some South African
    whose fingernails were checked at dusk
for a speck of gold. Your face
    blurs their brainy maps, & I apologize
for using their image of you this way,
    as if we agreed to rendezvous
among twelve misty stations of the cross.
    I run my hands through blond hair
till I own the store, my slender fingers
    toying with silver latches & the glint
of diamonds. I know you are a good man
    who worked & squirreled away coins
for small dreams, unable to stop seeing her
    wearing this necklace, a secret wad
of dollars pressed against your bad
    heart. Their cameras never aim at me,
Mister Decoy. I play with a sapphire brooch
    as if I'm one of Pindar's Graces

or Charites, but I live for the fit & tug
    of blue jeans as my hips sway to *ooh-*
la-la. I never clutch my foolish purse
    when you pass. Texas pours out
my mouth, & I know how to reach so my skirt
    rides up my thighs. The mink collar
of my cashmere sweater blinks its jade
    eyes. Years ago Jennifer dared me, & now
it's habit woven into flesh, Mister Decoy,
    & sometimes I can't stop myself
from clowning with the light this way.

Darling, my daddy's razor strop
is in my hands, & there's a soapy cloud
on my face. I'm a man of my word.
Didn't I say, If Obama's elected,
I'll shave off this damn beard
that goes back to '68, to Chicago?
I know, I also said I'd kiss the devil,
but first let me revise this contract.
I can taste tear gas. I hear a blur
of billy clubs when I hit the drums.
I haven't witnessed this mug shot
in decades, but I'm facing the mirror.
I'm still the same man. Almost.
Led Zeppelin is still in my nogginbox.
Alan Watts, old guru of ghosts
& folksingers, I can still two-step
& do-si-do to Clifton Chenier.
But, in no time, this philosopher
will be going down the drain, baby.
Look at how a finely honed razor works.
I may be a taxi driver, but I know time
opens an apple seed to find a worm.
See, I told you, my word is gold,
good as making a wager against
the eternal hush. The older I get

the quicker Christmas comes,
but if I had to give up the heavenly
taste of Guinness dark, I couldn't
live another goddamn day. Darling,
you can chisel that into my headstone.

THE EMPEROR OF

WATER CLOCKS

THE LAND OF COCKAIGNE

A drowned kingdom rises at daybreak
& we keep trudging on. A silhouette rides
the rope swing tied to a spruce limb,
the loudest calm in the marsh. Look
at the sinkholes, the sloped brokenness,
a twinned rainbow straddling the rocks.
See how forgiving—how brave nature is.
She drags us through teeming reeds
& turns day inside out, getting up
under blame, gazing at the horizon
as a throaty sparrow calls the raft home.
A wavering landscape is our one foothold.
Are we still moving? This old story
behind stories turns an epic season
a tangle of roses moved by night soil.
The boar, congo snake, & earthworm
eat into pigweed. The middle ground
is a flotilla of stars, a peacock carousel
& Ferris wheel spinning in the water
as vines unstitch the leach-work of salt,
thick mud sewn up like bodies fallen
into a ditch, blooming, about to erupt.
Water lily & spider fern. I see the tip
of a purple mountain, but sweetheart,
if it weren't for your late April kisses
I would have turned around days ago.

A box of tooth wheels sits on an ebony hippopotamus
made to count seasons. I show you a sketch of the float,
how it steals wet kisses out of a mouth, the bulbous belly
swollen with hours, my left hand at the hem of your skirt.
How many fallen empires dwell here triggered by a sundial,
revolutions & rebirths? I'm in a reverie again, my face
pressed against the rounded glass wall of the city aquarium
as hippopotami glide slowly through water, in sync to a tune
on my headphones. Why can't I stop intoning the alchemist
who used the clock to go between worlds & turn lead to gold?
A replica of this in a brothel in Athens once counted off
minutes each client spent in a room. If this is a footnote
to how one defines a day, no one knows this timepiece
as well as the superintendent of water debiting farmers.
The dark-green figs ripen under moonlight. Migratory
birds lift from shoulders of scarecrows at sunrise & arrive
in a new kingdom at sunset, true as the clock's escapement
mechanism. The bridge of zodiac signs moves across the top.
A lifetime poises in my fingers on the silver clasp of your bra
as spring's rapaciousness nears. Your slip drops to the floor
& ripples at our feet as a day-blooming cereus opens.
All the sweet mechanics cleave heaven & earth,
& a pinhole drips seconds through bronze.

THE EMPEROR

The tablet he inherited was encased
in leather, & in sleep he whispered
a decree to conquer the hermaphrodite
on the throne. Acacias touched yellow
to the night & peace reigned a decade.
When he ordered his brother to serve
as his double, his mother said, Son,
your father would have banished you
to the salt mines. The look in his eyes
was what Grotowski tried to capture
at La MaMa, a looped robe at his feet
& baroque notes echoing in his head.
The three double-jointed stuntmen
& master of props were his friends,
& he learned all the pressure points
from the third guard. He was emperor
before a script, a taste for honeycomb
at birth, long before the abominable
oath was tattooed on his forehead.
His brother would face the throng
mornings outside the marketplace
across from the old sacred abattoir
to sing bygones & lines of succession.
This was a place of drawn daggers
& acts of sedition, renown for blood

on stones & laments scribed on air,
& also for wheels drawing water
up rocky inclines to his garden.
He was born to claim his father's
flame trees & the white rhinoceros.
In another life, he could have been
an illustrious actor, a kind word
even for dumb brutes of the forest.
He mastered sublimity & decorum
bathed in the glow of a leading lady,
& the peach brandy & plum bread
he loved was always first tasted
by his double. Questions of fidelity
& bloodline, honor & dishonor, all
went back to Hagar & a gold scepter.
His brother was forbidden a name.
From his court he could see faces
lined up to praise his terraced garden
of shrubs, herbs, ornamental grasses,
& hues to bribe the raven to his door.
He said, Mother, time will forgive me
because I have always loved beauty.

THE FOOL

C'mon, Your Majesty, her brother?
I know the scent of belladonna
can poison a mind, even a king's,
but would you dare to behead
your own nightmares? Now,
I hope you are more than pewter
& pallor. Where is the early heart
I gladly remember from the days
I hailed as your father's cutthroat?
I know hearsay can undo a kingdom.
I never cursed your tower guards
& I dare translate their foofaraw.
I double-swear on the good book
though I could be our Shagspere
or William Kempe paying his tab
with a proud penny & a plug nickel.
Your Highness, only a horsewhip
could heal my unnatural tongue,
that is, if you consent to be the first
flogged up & down the castle steps.
After the guillotine & a coronation,
you would think a king too weak
to properly father a son & heir,
in the unholy days of the masque.
My queen, today, my lovely queen

singing wildly behind an iron door,
her head ready for your oak block,
holds now her lame bird in a box
of twigs, a toy against eternity.

THE KING'S SALT

The miners dressed in monkish garb
    led horses deep into briny catacombs
hewn by ancient rain. The horses crunched
    green apples while paced through a maze
of looped ropes, & the huge wooden pulleys
    & winches began to groan, moving blocks
& barrels of salt. The men were handpicked
    by the king, & the dark horses soon forgot
the pastures, walking circles, never to know
    the horizon again, wet grass under hooves.
If a miner died at home in bed beside his wife
    could another hand holding an apple or two
draw the horse into the rote, winding circle,
    obedient & unthinking? The penitents
held long poles with flame to burn off methane
    in the ceiling, the others pushed daylong
squat carts called the Hungarian dog.
    Faces & shapes rose from the monolith.
Here's a gnome, the guardian of miners,
    & this St. Kinga's Chapel, chandeliers
hanging—carved from a threefold silence.
    Wooden gutters drained off centuries
before shadows of German warplanes
    floated on the lakes of brine, hidden
by imperial weather. Now one stands

wondering if a king, for the hell of it,
touched royal crystals with his tongue
down in the dank half darkness,
or gazed within, to have seen firsthand
the moment when one carefully places
a small lamp behind a bust of salt.

As you can see, he first mastered light
& shadow, faces moving between grass
& stone, the beasts wading to the ark,
& then *The Decline of the Carthaginian
Empire*, before capturing volcanic reds,
but one day while walking in windy rain
on the Thames he felt he was descending
a hemp ladder into the galley of a ship,
down in the swollen belly of the beast
with a curse, hook, & a bailing bucket,
into whimper & howl, into piss & shit.
He saw winds hurl sail & mast pole
as the crewmen wrestled slaves dead
& half dead into a darkened whirlpool.
There it was, groaning. Then the water
was stabbed & brushed till voluminous,
& the bloody sharks were on their way.
But you're right, yes, there's still light
crossing the divide, seething around
corners of the thick golden frame.

The shadow knows. Okay. But what is this, the traveler's tail curled like a question mark, a tribe on her back? Snow falls among the headstones. The fat flakes curtain three worlds. In Southern folklore, they exhume the old world before skulking out to a new frontier of city lights. They live by playing dead. Bounty of lunacy. Bounty of what it seems. No, I'm not talking about lines stolen into a rock 'n' roll song. No, archsentimentalist, I'm not speaking of moonlight or a girl of wanderlust in a desert. But that's not a bad guess. I'm lost in your obscure imagination. Speaking of the dead, you know, Yeats also knew a little something about the occult. Sleepwalking is another story. Yes, the blank space says, Wake up, knucklehead, & listen to this: You might be getting onto something here. If I had different skin, would you read me differently, would you see something in the snow that isn't in the snow, something approaching genius? Would you press your nude body against the pages & try reading something into the life of the speaker? Would you nibble at the edges of my nightmares, & wake with the taste of death in your mouth, or would you open your eyes, lost in a field of hyacinth? Well, on a night like this, snow has fallen into my dreams. Lithium or horse could be a clue, but not necessarily so. Or, think of the two men aiming their dueling pistols—the years of silence between them— Alexander Pushkin falling into the January whiteness of history.

Charles, I'm also a magpie collecting every scrap
of song, color, & prophecy beside the river
in the lonesome valley, along the Trail of Tears,
switchbacks, demarcation lines, & railroad tracks,
over a ridge called the Devil's Backbone,
winding through the double-green of Appalachia
down to shady dominion & Indian summer.
I don't remember how many times,
caught between one divine spirit & the next
detour, I wanted to fly home the old way,
around contours of doubt, tailspins
I'd learned to gauge so well, voices
ahead, before, not yet born, & beyond,
doubling back to the scent of magnolia.
Whatever it was in the apparitional light
held us to the road. But your early sky
was different from mine, as I drifted up
from bottomland, snagged by grab vines
& bullfrog lingo in a bluesy grotto. One way
or another, a rise & fall is a rise & fall, a way in
& a way out, till we're grass danced-down.
I, too, know my Hopkins (Lightnin' & Gerard Manley),
gigging to this after-hours when all our little civil wars
unheal in the body. I shake my head till snake eyes fall
on the ground, as history climbs into the singing skull

to ride shotgun. Our days shaped by unseen movement
in the landscape, coldcocked by brightness coming
over a hill, wild & steady as a palomino runagate
spooked by something in the trees unsaid.
The redbud followed us into starless cities
& shook us out like dusty rags in a dizzy breeze.
But we're lucky we haven't been shaken down
to seed corn in a ragged sack, looped & cinched tight,
lumps of dirt hidden in our coat pockets.
Charles, we came as folk songs,
blues, country & western, to bebop & rock 'n' roll,
our shadows hanging out bandaged-up & drawn
on a wall easing into night melody of "Po' Lazarus"
at the top & the bottom of day. Each step taken,
each phrase, every snapped string, fallen arch,
& kiss on a forgotten street in Verona or Paris
transported us back—back to hidden paths,
abandoned eaves, & haylofts where a half century
of starlings roosted, back to when we were lost
in our dream-headed, separate eternities,
searching till all the pieces fit together,
till my sky is no bluer than your sky.

ROCK ME, MERCY

The river stones are listening
because we have something to say.
The trees lean closer today.
The singing in the electrical woods
has gone dumb. It looks like rain
because it is too warm to snow.
Guardian angels, wherever you're hiding,
we know you can't be everywhere at once.
Have you corralled all the pretty wild
horses? The memory of ants asleep
in daylilies, roses, holly, & larkspur.
The magpies gaze at us, still
waiting. River stones are listening.
But all we can say now is,
Mercy, please, rock me.

ISLANDS

An island is one great eye
      gazing out, a beckoning lighthouse,
searchlight, a wishbone compass,
      or counterweight to the stars.
When it comes to outlook & point
      of view, a figure stands on a rocky ledge
peering out toward an archipelago
      of glass on the mainland, a seagull's
wings touching the tip of a high wave,
      out to where the brain may stumble.

But when a mind climbs down
      from its lone craggy lookout
we know it is truly a stubborn thing,
      & has to leaf through pages of dust
& light, through pre-memory & folklore,
      remembering fires roared down there
till they pushed up through the seafloor
      & plumes of ash covered the dead
shaken awake worlds away, & silence
      filled up with centuries of waiting.

Sea urchin, turtle, & crab
　　came with earthly know-how,
& one bird arrived with a sprig in its beak,
　　before everything clouded with cries,
a millennium of small deaths now topsoil
　　& seasons of blossoms in a single seed.
Light edged along salt-crusted stones,
　　across a cataract of blue water,
& lost sailors' parrots spoke of sirens,
　　the last words of men buried at sea.

Someone could stand here
　　contemplating the future, leafing
through torn pages of St. Augustine
　　or the prophecies by fishermen,
translating spore & folly down to taproot.
　　The dreamy-eyed boy still in the man,
the girl in the woman, a sunny forecast
　　behind today, but tomorrow's beyond
words. To behold a body of water
　　is to know pig iron & mother wit.

Whoever this figure is,
　　he will soon return to dancing
through the aroma of dagger's log,
　　ginger lily, & bougainvillea,
between chants & strings struck
　　till gourds rally the healing air,
& the church-steeple birds
　　fly sweet darkness home.
Whoever this friend or lover is,
　　he intones redemptive harmonies.

To lie down in remembrance
      is to know each of us is a prodigal
son or daughter, looking out beyond land
      & sky, the chemical & metaphysical
beyond falling & turning waterwheels
      in the colossal brain of damnable gods,
a Eureka held up to the sun's blinding eye,
      born to gaze into fire. After conquering
frontiers, the mind comes back to rest,
      stretching out over the white sand.

LATITUDES

If I am not Ulysses, I am
his dear, ruthless half brother.
Strap me to the mast
so I may endure night sirens
singing my birth when water
broke into a thousand blossoms
in a landlocked town of the South,
before my name was heard
in the womb-shaped world
of deep sonorous waters.
Storms ran my ship to the brink,
& I wasn't myself in a kingdom
of unnamed animals & totem trees,
but never wished to unsay my vows.
From the salt-crusted timbers
I could only raise a battering ram
or cross, where I learned God
is rhythm & spores. If I am
Ulysses, made of his words
& deeds, I swam with sea cows
& mermaids in a lost season,
ate oysters & poisonberries
to approach the idea of death
tangled in the lifeline's slack

on that rolling barrel of a ship,
then come home to more than just
the smell of apples, the heavy oars
creaking the same music as our bed.

THE RELIC

In Saint Helena darkness falls into a window.
Napoleon tells the doctor to cut out his heart
& send it to the empress, Marie-Louise,

but not one word is said about his penis.
Had an auctioneer or bibliophile known
the weight or the true cost of infamy?

After his body was shipped home for burial
in a great hall of clocks & candelabra
few could reign over imperial silence.

One was Vignali, paid in silver forks, knives,
& 100,000 francs to curate the funeral,
whose manservant, Ali, confessed the deed.

Now, we ask time to show us the keepsake,
to let us see the proof in blue morocco
& velvet locked in a glass case.

I wonder if the urologist in Englewood,
New Jersey, wrapped it in raw silk
& placed the talisman under his bed.

Or if it became a study for a master of clones
rehearsing doxology & transubstantiation,
not even a murmur covered by swanskin.

It's a hint of the imagination awakened,
a shoelace, a dried-up fig or sea horse
awaiting the gallop of soundless waves.

ET TU, BRUTE?

They left the Second City
after years of stand-up & improv,
& came here to search faces
in crowds, on boulevards
& subways, & audition
for roles at a level of slow
pain that pulled them apart,
though they both perfected
Jerry & Peter before learning
betrayal doesn't always taste
like metal. Walking the same
street, one went to Red Hook
to live in a fifth-floor walk-up
where he burned sandalwood,
& the other to a girlfriend
he met on the set of a soap
living across from Central Park.
They would see each other
at galleries in SoHo & Chelsea,
& joke about days of free wine
& bread, or meet in a lobby
or the toilet at the Public,
reading the faintest graffiti
over the urinal, & one wanted
to point out to the other how

it was usually the businessman
in a suit or Judas in a top hat
who didn't wash his hands.
They were in *Game of Thrones*
on HBO, but one fell in love
with Jack Daniel's & the other
began working comedy clubs,
& seldom spoke of life & death
floating between them. One
afternoon in mid-September
they sat across from each other
in Washington Square Park
as strangers strolled & a quartet
played "My Favorite Things,"
& one said to himself, No,
that can't be him, because
he's two years older than me,
& the second said to his mutt,
I knew the day would come
when one of us sees the other
dead on a foreign street.

THE GOLD PISTOL

There's always someone who loves gold
bullion, boudoirs, & bathtubs, always
some dictator hiding in a concrete culvert
crying, Please don't shoot, a high priest
who mastered false acts & blazonry,
the drinking of a potion after bathing
in slow oils of regret, talismans, & amulets
honed to several lifetimes of their own,
the looting of safes & inlaid boxes of jewels,
moonlight on brimstone, fires eating sky,
& this is why my heart almost breaks
when a man dances with Gaddafi's pistol
raised over his head, knowing the sun
runs to whatever shines, & as the young
grows old, there's always a raven
laughing on an iron gatepost.

A war's going on somewhere, but tonight
a forest glows beneath the big top,
calling for the sword swallower & contortionist,
the beautiful high-wire walker who almost dies
nightly, the fire eater, the lion tamer, the believer
of sage & sleeping salts who wears a money belt
against her Icelandic skin. A drunk wants to be healed
by contagious laughter or a shot through the heart
by an old lover who lives in King of Prussia.
Three months ago, before Caldonia's body
was found by the police in waist-high weeds,
birds sang here. Maybe her killer is now
throwing a baseball to knock a dummy
into the water barrel, or buying cotton candy
for his daughter, or circling a bull elephant.
Who can remember the woman, the sirens,
her mother fainting next to this beaten tree?
Nighthawks work a lit thread through the evening.
The calliope makes the air tinny.
The strongman presses six hundred pounds,
his muscles flexed for the woman
whose T-shirt says THESE GUNS ARE LOADED.
But one minute later he's on the ground,
a petite bystander giving him mouth-
to-mouth. A cop blows his shiny whistle,

trying to clear a path for the paramedics.
Teenagers slurp root beer floats
& munch corn dogs, after they've leaned
into each other's arms in the flipped-over,
high-spinning rides, & have fallen in love
for the second time in three weeks.

MINOTAUR

He circled the roundabout
of bullheaded desires, lost in the maze
among broken icons, traces of blood
& sunflower seed left on numbered stones.

He was taller than a man,
tall as a honey locust at the end of an alley.
He slipped a knot, a sword at the equinox,
& entered the village plaza, hooking the air
& wheeling in circles.

The night dropped her cape,
& then artisans were ordered
to strike the figure onto a coat of arms
& gold coins. His cock & nose ring.
The triple-six tattooed on his rump.
Roses etched their scent on the night.

TORSION

He was in waist-high grass. An echo of a voice
     searched for him as he crawled along a ditch,
the greenhorn's blood reddening the mud, & the scent
     of burnt Cosmoline. *What's the spirit of the bayonet,*
soldier? His mind the mouth of a cave, the horizon
     was nitrate as he walked on his hands,
a howl in the crosshairs, rain tapping his helmet.
     He had been tapered, honed, & polished in AIT,
& then pointed toward grid coordinates on a ragged map,
     his feelings cauterized, & now a glint of wet light
touches the sniper's rifle in a grove of jackfruit.
     Silence, a stone in his belly, an anvil on his head.
What's the spirit of the bayonet, soldier? He dove on the pig
     & his body became part of the metal, tracer rounds
scorched the living air, the dirt & sky, & the edges of night
     approached. Only his fingers would recall threading
another belt of ammo. He didn't wish to know how many
     shadows hugged the ground. No, he couldn't stop
firing as he rode the M60 machine gun to a primal grunt
     before he buckled & spewed vomit over the barrel,
the torsion a whiplash of hues. *What's the spirit*
     of the bayonet, soldier? After medevac choppers
flew out the badly wounded & the body bags,
     three men in his squad became two tigers at sunset

& walked through the village. They kicked a pagoda
        till it turned into the crumbly dust of cinnabar,
& then torched thatched roofs. The captain's citation
        never said how fear tussled him in the paddy ditch,
& the star in its velvet-lined box was a scarab
        in a pharaoh's brain. The dead visited nightly.
The company chaplain blessed him, but he'd sit hours
        gazing out at the sea & could never bless himself.
The battalion saluted but he wished to forget his hands,
        & the thought of metal made him stand up straight.
He shipped back to the world only to remember blood
        on the grass, men dancing on a lit string of bullets,
women & children wailing among the flame trees,
        & he wished he hadn't been trained so damn well.
What's the spirit of the bayonet, soldier? He was back
        now, back to where he brandished fronds as swords
to guard their tree house, his mama at church
        singing hallelujah, his daddy in Lucky's
swigging Falstaff. He kept thinking of his cousin Eddie
        who drove his girl to Galveston in a Chevy pickup,
"California Dreamin'" looping through the cab.
        He could still see round fishing boats on the edge
of the South China Sea, a woman's long black hair
        falling in a rising wave, moonlight on the skin
of sappers, their bodies wound in concertina.
        He switches off his blue transistor radio
& walks straight into pines along the Black Warrior,
        searching for arrowheads, bagging rabbit & quail.
He's back to the Friday his draft card came, when he first

mastered a willful blindness, back to outsmarting prey,
& he duckwalks across the clearing under power lines.
    Now ashamed of something naked as a good question
redbirds flash in a counterambush. *Thou shalt not kill*
    echoes across clay hills miles from his loved ones,
& he slouches deeper into the Choctaw's old growth,
    through a hoop of light, away from a face stealing
his brother's, so deep he can hardly hear himself plead
    to shiny crows in a weeping willow.

FORTRESS

Now I begin with these two hands
held before me as blessing & weapon,

blackbirds in fierce flight & instruments
of touch & consolation. This sign means

stop, & this one of course means come forth,
friend. I draw a circle in the red iron clay

around my feet, where no evil spirit dares
to find me. One's hands held at this angle

over a boy's head are a roof over a sanctuary.
I am a greenhorn in my fortress in the woods

with my right eye pressed to a knothole.
I can see a buzz in the persimmon tree,

its ripe letting go—a tiny white cross
in each seed. The girl's fiery jump rope

strikes the ground. I see the back door
of that house close to the slow creek

where a drunken, angry man stumbles
across the threshold every Friday.

I see forgiveness, unbearable twilight,
& these two big hands know too much

about nail & hammer, plank & uneasy sky.
Hewn stone & mortar is another world,

& sometimes a tall gate comes first.
Then huge wooden barrels of grain,

flour, salted meat, & quicklime before
twenty-eight crossbows in four towers.

LONGITUDES

Before zero meridian at Greenwich
Galileo dreamt Dante on a ship
& his beloved Beatrice onshore,
both holding clocks, drifting apart.

His theory was right even if
he couldn't steady the ship
on rough seas beyond star charts
& otherworldly ports of call.

"But the damn blessed boat
rocked, tossing sailors to & fro
like a chorus of sea hags
in throes of ecstasy."

My whole world unmoors
& slips into a tug of high tide.
A timepiece faces the harbor—
a fixed point in a glass box.

You're standing on the dock.
My dreams of you are oceanic,
& the Door of No Return
opens a galactic eye.

If a siren stations herself
between us, all the clocks
on her side, we'll find each other
sighing our night song in the fog.

The round, hanging lanterns,
lit faces in a window of the Marble Palace
Catherine the Great built for a lover,
with the Field of Mars below,
snow falling inside two minds.
One translated Babylonian folktales
so the other could stand in line early morning
for bread at the House of Scholars.
A touch of dawn was again nightfall,
their room furnished with scattered papers,
rare books, a couch with springs poking out,
a bookcase, a floral pitcher, a china cabinet,
a naked light bulb dangling over a table.
Did the two poets learn it took more
to sing & reflect the burning icy stars
of poetry where privilege & squalor
lived beneath the same ornate ceiling?
Did they tiptoe from the wintery dusk
of the servants' wing, follow the pseudo-
Gothic stairs up to the forbidden aromas
of Turkish tobacco, sugar, & exotic teas?
Sometimes, they kept themselves warm
with talk of the empress's love of horses
as they galloped another century. Then,

sketches of their time at the Stray Dog
lit the air around those neoclassic nights,
& maybe they also spoke about "Venice
rotting with gold" near the Arctic Circle,
& anger almost kept them warm on days
they bent over pages of snow blindness
where tears brought them to laughter.

Ito ran to a window. He danced.
He howled. He cursed the moon,
interned in a camp before he was
carted on a ship back to Tokyo.
Hadn't he almost died for art
the evenings he ate bread soup?
If he wished to forget those days
& nights dancing in drawing rooms
in London, or translating Fenollosa's
notes on Noh, he'd have to unbraid
himself from *At the Hawk's Well*,
& then let go of the Egyptian
mask Dulac painted him into—
claws, beak, feathers, & legend.
Why did that silly boy tell a story
about his grandmother weeping
when she first saw him dressed
in his grandfather's samurai armor
to hold the gaze of Lady Cunard?
He was again studying the fox
holding a biscuit in his hand,
saying, "I went to a great hill
in Hampstead & I made my soul
into the soul of the fox." Finally,
he would let go of his Europe,

& not think of those he loved
& taught, Isadora lost. Now,
powerless & alone, he dances
his ten steps again & again,
wanting to know if a hawk
could peck the eyes out of a fox.

CAFFE REGGIO

They clink glasses of Merlot & joke
in a metalanguage among friends
about early autumn in a gulag
of lonely washes. Then one says,
Ivan the Terrible was a teenage vampire
who fell in love with art & soothsayers,
& another says, If he had only ridden
a gondola through the canals of Venice
once or twice, they could have civilized
the madman dreaming of the Baltics.
Then, one of them says something
about sentimentality being the death
of imagination, metaphor, & foreplay.
They are one small republic of ideas,
three good friends, & almost one mind
when they lift their eyes to greet
a woman walking in from the day's
blinding array of disorder & chance.
She finds a table at the corner window,
orders a bowl of fruit & cappuccino,
opens a copy of *Watermark*, presses
down the pages, breaking the spine.
The three sit, smiling at each other,
& Derek says, I wonder if she knows
Joseph still picks up his mail here.

KRAR

We have this to call to the dead
among the living, this wooden triangle,
its belly a gourd-resonator
the size of a man's cupped hands
inverted, in prayer & war.
It throws sorrow & laughter
against the eardrum
till the silent motion of the hills
finds us in the city.
Water trembles at the taproot
when strings are struck,
reaching down through muscle memory
to a shelter of mud bricks baked under
three thousand years of sunlight,
from the goatherd to the King
of Kings, to Bob Marley. If Ethiopia
opens in the long Egyptian trumpets
or natural blues of the saxophone,
there's little pomp & circumstance
in this earthy instrument
raised between violin & crossbow,
to dance with, or embrace.
When it speaks, especially
to the drum, this sounding-loom
is the voice of a nation
bargaining with the gods.

In a half-broken room of the hospice
the bent figure on a bed is far from Osibisa
or his twenty-four-hour rock 'n' roll gig
in England. Now, fame is a tale mermaids
tell fishermen, but all I want to know is
where are Kiki Djan's friends & lovers,
his millions? His eyes stop us at the foot
of the bed. Outside, migratory birds
fly in the shape of a falling garment.
He hugs a tape recorder, head swaying
to an unreleased recording cut overseas.
The hum of an insect can hold his gaze
for hours, the ancestors at a side door.
The song is his only possession, fingers
on the keyboard only a little howl lost
in a trade wind nudging a pirate ship.
His eyes tell us all the tangled paths
taken, & now he must be a Lindbergh
who crossed the sleepless Atlantic.
To fully master out-of-body travel
by dead reckoning, one has to know
all the overtime shadows of obeah
working around the clock in Accra.
He stares at the buzz of a bluebottle
throbbing against the windowpane.

A NIGHT IN TUNISIA

How long have I listened
to this blues & how long
has Dizzy Gillespie been dead?
I remember an old longing,
a young man reaching
for luck, a finger poised
between pages of Baldwin's
Notes of a Native Son, a clock
stopped for a hard, crystal-
clear moment. This was
a lifetime before the night
streets of Tunisia burned
on cell phones in the clouds,
tear gas & machine-gun fire
& my head in my hands
an hour. I traveled there
many times, humble
side streets & sweetness
of figs, hot seasons of meat
on the bone, naked feeling,
& Dizzy's horn still ablaze,
a bleat of big fat notes
in the dark. Even if I'd never
stepped above simple laws,
my youth had betrayed me
with years still to come
& jasmine in bloom.

The kneeling figure is from Yama or Carthage,
& I ask, What was his worth in gold, in salt,
spices, statuary, or commemorated axioms?
L, if we weren't brave enough to believe
we could master time, we wouldn't have
locked hands with old gods smelted down
in shops where crosses were etched above doors,
pressed into the coinage of a new empire,
& palm readers flogged in the market.
But of course there sits Marcus Aurelius
with stoic meditations on a borrowed tongue,
gazing out at sublime poppies, an eternal
battlefield, his hand extended as a scepter
over the piazza where his bronze horse
cantered up onto Michelangelo's pedestal
carved from marble steps of the temple
of Castor & Pollux, & we wait for him
to outflank the epochs of wind & rain.
L, everything around here is an epitaph.
Even the light. This morning, squinting out
a window as rays play off a stone cistern,
I hear someone whisper, "Waste no time
arguing about what a good man should be,
the worms will give us their verdict

by nightfall." I don't know who said this,
but today, love, I'm brave enough to say,
Antiquity, here's my barbarian shadow
squatting under the horse's raised right hoof.

ODE TO THE OUD

Gourd-shaped muse swollen
with wind in the mulberry,
tell me everything you're made of,
little desert boat of Ra.
Oblong box of Bedouin doves
pecking pomegranate seeds out of the air,
you're the poet's persona, his double
in the high priest's third chamber,
each string a litany of stars over the Sahara.
Pear-shaped traveler, strong but so light,
is there a wishbone holding you together?
I wish I knew how to open you up
with an eagle's feather or a pick
whittled from buffalo horn,
singing alive the dust of Nubia.
Rosewood seasoned long ago,
I wish I could close your twelve mouths
with kisses. Tongues strung in a row,
I wish I could open every sound in you.
I envy one blessed to master himself
by rocking you in his lonely arms.
Little ship of sorrow, bend your voice
till the names of heroes & courtesans,
birds & animals, prayers & love songs,
swarm from your belly.

ENVOY TO PALESTINE

I've come to this one grassy hill
in Ramallah, off Tokyo Street,
to place a few red anemones
& a sheaf of wheat on Darwish's grave.
A borrowed line transported me beneath
a Babylonian moon & I found myself
lucky to have the shadow of a coat
as warmth, listening to a poet's song
of Jerusalem, the hum of a red string
Caesar stole off Gilgamesh's lute.
I know a prison of sunlight on the skin.
The land I come from they also dreamt
before they arrived in towering ships
battered by the hard Atlantic winds.
Crows followed me from my home.
My coyote heart is an old runagate
redskin, a noble savage, still Lakota,
& I knew the bow before the arch.
I feel the wildflowers, all the grasses
& insects singing to me. My sacred dead
is the dust of restless plains I come from,
& I love when it gets into my eyes & mouth
telling me of the roads behind & ahead.
I go back to broken treaties & smallpox,
the irony of barbed wire. Your envoy

could be a reprobate whose inheritance
is no more than a swig of firewater.
The sun made a temple of the bones
of my tribe. I know a dried-up riverbed
& extinct animals live in your nightmares
sharp as shark teeth from my mountains
strung into this brave necklace around
my neck. I hear Chief Standing Bear
saying to Judge Dundy, "I am a man,"
& now I know why I'd rather die a poet
than a warrior, tattoo & tomahawk.

TIMBUKTU

I sing an elegy for the city of 333 saints,
for every crumbling mosque & minaret,
for the libraries standing for centuries
against dust storms, for the nomads
herding trees of life across the desert
along trails where camels hauled salt
to rafts woven on the river Niger
before the empire of Songhai fell.
The griots speak of an epic memory
of stardust in sand, but now mercenaries
kidnap, run drugs, & kill in bold daylight.
Blood money brought them into Libya,
& more blood money took them home
brandishing stolen guns & grenades.
When Lord Byron intones in *Don Juan*
"Where geography finds no one to oblige her"
I hear my name. But no one stands up
to prophecies the other side of limbo
against the modern as a metallic eye
drones overhead. Medieval clouds
may promise safe passage or escape
routes out of Mali, but the God-fearing
cannot remember the faces of death
after kicking in all the drums.

GHAZAL, AFTER FERGUSON

Somebody go & ask Biggie to orate
what's going down in the streets.

No, an attitude is not a suicide note
written on walls around the streets.

Twitter stays lockstep in the frontal lobe
as we hope for a bypass beyond the streets,

but only each day bears witness
in the echo chamber of the streets.

Grandmaster Flash's thunderclap says
he's not the grand jury in the streets,

says he doesn't care if you're big or small
fear can kill a man on the streets.

Take back the night. Take killjoy's
cameras & microphones to the streets.

If you're holding the hand lightning strikes
juice will light you up miles from the streets

where an electric chair surge dims
all the county lights beyond the streets.

Who will go out there & speak laws
of motion & relativity in the streets?

Yusef, this morning proves a crow
the only truth serum in the street.

INTERROGATION

He picks till it grows
into a tiny butterfly,
a transfigured bee-
shaped wound,
& then into a secret icon
filled with belief,
bloody philosophy,
& a drop of stardust.

A moment of half-
dead radiance
pulses on his skin
till his mouth closes
on a phrase in Latin,
& he wonders if an oath
leaves a scar.

He can't hear
the nightlong voice
recant in the bell tower,
or the wasp's torn wings
lifting hints of light
in the spider's web.

When thought is
tissue, or a string
of dust that sings for rain,
unforgivable hours
divide into testimonies
delivered by the wind,
saying, Forget.

He tries not to pick
at the mute evidence
of the recent past,
letting pop songs
bleed over him
on the radio.

He lifts the scab
with a fingernail,
till the almost healed
opens its little doubtful
mouth of resignation,
till he can gaze down
into himself & see
where eternity begins.

PRECIOUS METALS

After the MRI & robot
made of precious metals,
some heretical go-between
shouted all the tautologies
& fruitless apologies to the planet.
I came to you, saying, Please
look into my eyes & tap a finger
against my heart to undo
every wrong I've ever done,
every infraction done to me
in the country of crab apple
& honeysuckle. I want to
toy with each blade of grass
& ripening plum, to suck the
last salutation from doubt,
& mount a dancer's platform.
I've outlived silent seasons
whipped bloody & ransomed.
But let us ride the big wheel
into dawn, a naked kiss.
I say, If you wish to trouble
my persona or need to break
my bones to show me mercy,
then get on with your work
& fix me the way a Delta blues
fixes a muddy river's night sky.

A PRAYER

Great Ooga-Booga, in your golden pavilion
beside the dung heap, please
don't let me die in a public place.
I still see the man on the café floor
at the airport beneath a canopy
of fluorescence, somewhere
in the Midwest or back east,
travelers walking around him
& texting on cell phones
while someone shocked him back,
fiddling with dials & buttons
on a miraculous instrument.
Was the memory of a dress in his head?

Great Ooga-Booga, forgive me
for wearing out my tongue before
I said your praises. No, I haven't
mastered the didgeridoo.
I don't have an epic as a bribe.
My words are simple. Please
don't let me die gazing up at a streetlight
or the Grand Central facades.
Let me go to my fishing hole
an hour before the sun sinks
into the deep woods, or swing
on the front porch, higher & higher
till I'm walking on the ceiling.

He blows a ram's horn at the first gate of the third kingdom, & one would swear it sounds like questions in the air. He walks down a troubadour's path that comes to a halt as if his song has broken in half, standing on cobblestones that stop before tall waves below. Whatever was here is now gone, except for a percussive whisper of mail & swords. He knows the sea is a keeper of records. Gazing up at the sun, he shakes his head & walks toward a refugee camp with a sack of beans, bread, dried tomatoes, & fish, where he plays "Hallelujah" on a toy trumpet. He knows they hate a bugle blown at dawn, or the sound of taps. A sloping path toward the center of town leads him to a prison made of river stones & thatch. The faces behind bars wait for him. Does he dare to raise his reed flute to his lips this mute hour? The sun sinks like a clarion, an old war cry across windy grass or questions in the air. He goes to the rear door of the slaughterhouse & plays his Pan fife till the flies go, as the workers speak of days they drank rose water. He heads down along the creek's muddy bank, finds a fallen tree, sits, & raises the clay flute to his lips. A magpie lands on a branch a foot away. He stops playing, whispers to his messenger, Okay, now go out there & tell them.

We have gone there, sitting here
while Herbie plays water on stone,
his piano among the misty trees.
Rainy light flows over hillocks
beside the sea, leaves, & high grass,
underneath nighttime till the Egg
glows. A place becomes the shape
of one's mind, & secretive animals
encounter us sleepwalkers. Dawn
flows over round wooden cisterns
atop buildings as East River fog
journeys along the streets & avenues.
All the seasons crowd here at once,
& each has several minds. The boy
never leaves the middle of my life.
The firebirds eat clouds of insects
as black keys counter white keys,
& I beg you to sing me an old song.
I weigh love of fruit in both hands.
We're two halves of a struck bell.
The boy's here, his big jolly balloon
tugging me now & then off-balance.
You wake me, laughing in your sleep.
The roots are knotted underneath us.
The boy smiles, & then dares me to kiss

my left elbow. You are a double mirror
guarding me from city lights & free will,
& I'm too scared to let go of your voice
in a subkingdom of mist on the stones.
Damned if we do. Damned if we don't.
The LP spins nightlong on repeat.
The boy has my long, girlish eyelashes.

FROM

REQUIEM

So,
when the strong unholy high winds
whiplashed over the sold-off marshlands
eaten back to a sigh of salt water,
the Crescent City was already shook down to her pilings,
her floating ribs, her spleen & backbone,
left trembling in her Old World facades
& postmodern lethargy, lost to waterlogged
memories & quitclaim deeds,
exposed for all eyes, damnable
gaze, plumb line & heartthrob,
ballast & water table,
already the last ghost song
gone, no more than a drunken curse
among oak & sweet gum leaves, a tally
of broken treaties & absences echoing
cries of birds over the barrier islands
inherited by the remittance man, scalawag,
& King Cotton, & already the sky
was falling in on itself,
calling like a cloud of seagulls
gone ravenous as the Gulf
reclaiming its ebb & flowchart
while the wind banged on shutters

& unhinged doors from their frames
& unshingled the low-ridged roofs
while the arch-believers hummed
"Precious Lord" & "Deep River"
as the horsehair plaster walls
galloped along with the surge,
already folklore began to rise up
from the buried lallygag & sluice
pulsing beneath the Big Easy
rolling between & through itself,
caught in some downward tug
& turn, like a world of love affairs
backed up in a stalled inlet,
a knelt-down army of cypress,
a testament to how men dreamt land
out of water, where bedrock
was only the heart's bump
& grind, its deep, dark churn
& acceleration, blowsy down
to those unmoored timbers,
already nothing but water
mumbling as the great turbulent eye
lingered on a primordial question,
then turned, the gauzy genitalia of Bacchus
& Zulu dangling in magnolias & rain trees,
& already *The Book of the Dead*
unfolded pages, & water rose
to leaf through the before
& after, the benedictions
& prayers spoken in tongues

rising in the tide of flotsam
& debris of fallen churches
across the Lower Ninth, slush
working its way up clapboard
& slave-brick walls of houses
tilted in a dirge, up the last rung
of the ladder, up to the voices
caught in an attic, & then stopped
in midair like a hundred washing
machines churning, & already
cries from a domed purgatory
broke from the storm within
where proxy armies clashed
on weekends, & for a moment,
as if we aren't here, demons ride
the shoulders of outlaw angels
through streets of an antiworld
where thieves of bread & milk
are clubbed to brick sidewalks
by keepers of the law as the levee's
uncorked boom drowns the solo
of Bolden's cornet driving a note
up the long river of rivers, saying,
I'm the mama & papa of ragtime,
& already a hush came to those
trapped behind barred windows
& waterlines measuring the sag
in the dragline as bottom fish
floated up, lost in the Big Muddy
unburying the wormy compost

of days rotting in the darkness,
& a windup toy inching along
crawfish mud & bloody slag,
& already they're turning pages
of the uncharted old lost seasons
footnoted in the abridged maps
warning of man-eating savages,
to Jean-Baptiste's flotilla of 6 ships
carrying 6 carpenters & 30 convicts
to rip out miles & miles of saw vines
& dig trenches, born to erect makeshift
shelters of raw sappy wood & speculate
on their stolen dreams, the engineer
Pierre Le Blond de la Tour saying, No,
not here, the river will never stop trying
to reclaim what's taken from her, even if
we build earthen walls to block her reach
because she will go around, under, or over,
& already the spine of their logbook
of calculations was broken & splayed
as newcomers hailed from far reaches
as pirates, woodsmen, & money changers
(all hard men), ready to claim coffin-girls
ferried in by high churches of France,
& already a thick wavy vein of ink
widens into midnight, into daybreak,
the wind drawing Audubon's ghost
through the almost gone, straggly
grass, out into the oily marsh bog
where disappearing land begs no footprint,

out to where hard evidence rainbows
up, leaving thousands hurting to be
counted as no more than sea turtle,
eel, brown pelican, egret, mud puppy, crab,
& already water wounds everything
into uncountable small deaths moored
in cypress, stinking up our springtime
with a pestilence going to the dark ages
on harbors where boats sway shifting light,
the dead talking to us from a masterpiece,
saying, We are forbidden to remember
we were defeated by what we devoured,
& already from a mile down plumes
keep rising up through weeks & months,
animal cries & the language of robots
where BP diving machines moonwalk,
surging as long-ago drowned shadows
of carrier pigeons drag up hellish silence,
& already the first "climate refugees"
are those who first built the aqueducts
to route fresh artesian springs from salt,
& now watch nature take back what was
stolen from them, treasuring know-how
passed down, who gather Gulf grasses
to weave baskets, whittle spirit totems
perfectly, train bird dogs, plot new stars
circling above mysteries of everyday lives,
& raising their small houses eight feet
high on pilings—as if some land bridge
to early Biloxi-Chitimacha-Choctaw—

who pick berries, trap rabbit & hunt deer
& quail, harvest crawdads, hook catfish
& gig fat bullfrogs, still singing to heal
wounds, still unable to leave their dead
who never surrendered, & already—

ACKNOWLEDGMENTS

Grateful acknowledgment is made to the following publications,
in which the new poems in this volume originally appeared:
Boston Review, Callaloo, The Fight & The Fiddle,
The New Yorker, Oxford American, PEN America,
Poem-a-Day, *Poetry, The Progressive, Smithsonian.*

Love in the Time of War was published as a fine-press
edition designed and printed by Robin Price.

"A World of Daughters" premiered with the
Trondheim Voices and Munich Chamber Orchestra, 2019.

An excerpt of "Requiem" was first published in
Angles of Ascent: A Norton Anthology of Contemporary
African American Poetry, W. W. Norton, 2013.

"The Candlelight Lounge" is for Larry Hilton.